Better Spread Betting

by Tony Loton

www.betterspreadbetting.com

Copyright © Tony Loton / LOTONtech Limited 2012.

This edition published by LOTONtech Limited (www.lotontech.com).

ISBN 978-0955989346

All rights reserved. No part of this publication may be reproduced or distributed in any form or by any means without the prior permission of the author and / or publisher.

The material in this book is provided for educational purposes only. No responsibility for loss occasioned to any person or corporate body acting or refraining to act as a result of reading material in this book can be accepted by the author or publisher. The author is not authorised to give financial advice.

All trademarks are the property of their respective owners. LOTONtech Limited is not associated with any product or vendor mentioned in this book except where stated. LOTONtech Limited is, or has been, an advertising affiliate for some of the spread betting companies mentioned, but your decision to use their services is entirely your own. Any mention of third party companies is not intended to imply their endorsement of the content of this book.

Unless otherwise stated; any third-party quotes, images and screenshots, or portions thereof, are included under 'fair use' for comment, news reporting, teaching, scholarship, and research.

Proofread by Becky Loton.

Contents

About the Book, page 5

About the Author, page 6

1 – Introduction to Financial Spread Betting, page 7

2 – Trading Timescales and Styles, page 27

3 – Opening an Account and Placing a Bet, page 45

4 – Tools of the Trade, page 61

5 – Tricks of the Trade, page 83

6 – Risk Doesn't Have To Be Risky, page 97

7 – Identifying Trading Opportunities, page 119

8 – One More Thing..., page 135

Appendix – Spread Betting Resources, page 145

About the Book

In May 2012 I initiated the "Better Spread Betting" project at www.betterspreadbetting.com as a vehicle for authoring a brand new no-nonsense yet comprehensive book about financial spread betting. The plan was to publish the warts 'n' all works-in-progress chapters on-line so that potential readers and other spread bettors could comment on them and link to them, with the view to making the "Better Spread Betting" book even better through reader involvement. As well as creating a book about better spread betting, I hoped to create a better book about spread betting; both theoretical and practical, and at all times accessible to a wide readership of differing skill levels. A tall order, I know.

Since I intended it to be so comprehensive, I thought about titling it the "Spread Betting Bible" or even the "Better Spread Betting Bible", but I decided not to alienate those potential readers who may be atheists, agnostics, or followers of non-monotheistic religions. So simply "Better Spread Betting" it is.

While I "keep it real" by mentioning several spread betting companies by name in the context of their (at the time of writing) particular features, I hope to have judged their offerings reasonably impartially on the basis of my use of their facilities rather than on the basis of which one of their advertisements gets the most clicks on my web site. In any case, my advice - not that I'm giving individual advice, you understand - would be to run with two or three of the spread betting companies at least until you have decided which one is right for you; and maybe even longer, as a hedge against putting all your eggs into one spread betting basket.

In this book I aim to challenge some of the commonly held beliefs about spread betting: that it is all about day trading exotic currencies and commodities, that it requires a lot of money to get started, or that it's risky and dangerous. All of those beliefs about spread betting can be true, but they don't have to be.

If you are reading this book in an electronic format such as Portable Document Format (PDF) you can jump straight to additional related content by clicking the hyperlinks that you will find throughout.

About the Author

Tony Loton is a private (but you wouldn't think so from his prolific writing) individual who trades his own money. He has never been directly involved in the finance industry except as an IT consultant and as a freelance financial journalist for publications including The Motley Fool (UK), the Financial-Spread-Betting.com web site (plus various others), and TRADERS' Magazine. Previously he had written for the Barclays Stockbrokers "Smart Investor" magazine, and he was once mentioned as a "day trader" in the Money section of the Sunday Times newspaper.

Tony's previous "best selling" (as in *his* best selling) books have included:

- Stop Orders published by Harriman House.

- Position Trading published by LOTONtech.

Please note that Tony Loton is not authorised to give financial or tax advice.

1 – Introduction to Financial Spread Betting

In this chapter I will start gently by telling you (or reminding you) what financial spread betting is, and how it is similar to - yet different from - traditional share dealing. If you're a seasoned spread bettor already, don't lose heart as there will be plenty of advanced material in later chapters. This introduction (for new spread bettors) or revision exercise (for existing spread bettors) will ensure that we're all starting with the same understanding of what financial spread betting is.

Before we begin, let me get something off my chest...

Gambling or Investing

Much of the traditional investment literature will lead you to believe that spread betting is the more dangerous poor relation of the more noble art of "investing". When you are spread betting, you are gambling, whereas when you are "investing" you are loyally backing British (or other) business based on your considered opinions about their prospects.

Don't believe it!

Spread betting is just another trading platform like a stock broker share dealing account, stocks-and-shares Individual Savings Account (ISA) or Self-Invested Personal Pension (SIPP). You can trade or "invest in" Barclays Bank shares (for example) using any of those platforms, and in every case you are hoping that you can sell the shares next week, next month, or next year, for more than what you paid for them. There are some subtle differences, which will be explained shortly, but in all cases you are taking the same speculative "gamble".

For the record, I am actually more "investment" than "day trader" oriented, and yet I prefer spread betting to traditional share dealing.

What is Financial Spread Betting?

In layman's terms financial spread betting is a tax-free* way of making money when the prices of equities (i.e. stocks or shares), stock indices (like the FTSE 100), commodities (like oil and gold) and currencies (like the US dollar) go up or down.

UK tax laws could change in the future.

You're not buying or selling "shares", you are simply placing a bet with a broker that the price of the stock (or other financial instrument) that you chose will rise or fall.

The word "spread" refers to the difference between the buying (ask or offer) and selling (bid) prices of the instrument you are betting on. It's like when you buy or sell a car and the dealer offers you a lower price to buy your car than the price he will charge someone else to buy it from him. That's how he makes his money, and that's how the spread betting companies make their money too. You might be able to buy (bet long) Vodafone shares at a price of 171p-per-share, but the spread betting company will only give you 170p-per-share (for example) when you want to sell them back. If those shares rise by 5p-per-share between you buying and selling them, to 175 / 176 then you have made a 4p-per-share profit and the spread betting company has taken the other 1p-per-share. In this case everyone is a winner, and the spread betting company almost always is a winner thanks to that 1p-per-share price differential or "spread".

Essential Differences between Spread Betting and Share Dealing

Unless you have a professional trading background, there's a good chance that you will be migrating to financial spread betting after first trying your hand at conventional share dealing. It is therefore important to understand the essential differences between spread betting and share dealing.

Pounds-per-Point, not Pounds Invested

The most significant difference between spread betting compared with share dealing via a traditional stockbroker, and one that may seem strange when you first make the transition, is that you bet in terms of pounds-per-point rather than "investing" an amount in pounds.

When you invest £1000 in Big Bank plc (not a real company), you stand to lose £1000 if the company goes bust regardless of the price you paid for the shares. When you spread bet £1-per-point on Big Bank plc, you would stand to lose £1000 if the shares were priced at 1000p-per-share when you placed the bet but a lower £500 if the shares were priced at 500p-per-share when you placed the bet. If you really wanted to "invest" the equivalent of £1000 using a spread bet on a 500p-per-share stock, you would need to place a bet at £2-per-point.

At any given time, the profit or loss on your spread bet is the amount that the price has moved up or down since you placed the bet multiplied by your £££-per-point stake, and this is the amount that you win or lose when you choose to close the bet. The following chart illustrates a sequence of spread bet trades in which the trader loses £19 on a £1-per-point spread bet (because the price falls by 19 points) and then wins £36 on a £2-per-point trade (because the price rises by 18 points on his double-size bet).

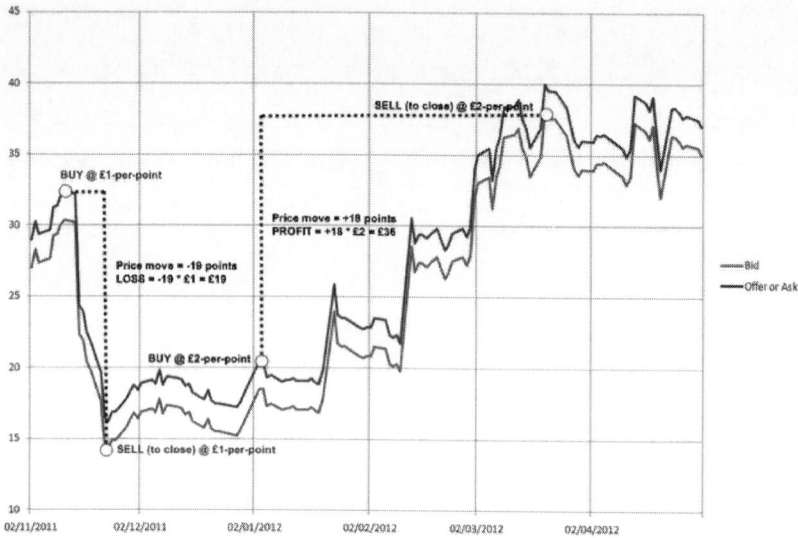

In those examples the price has actually moved by less than 19 points (down) and 18 points (up) respectively, but the trader has suffered the addition of the bid-ask spread that is indicated by the two parallel price lines; he always buys on the upper line and sells on the lower line. Oh, and this is not meant to be construed as an example of good trading; it's merely a hypothetical demonstration of how money is made or lost on a spread bet.

Leverage and Margin

To "invest" £1000 in a company via a traditional stockbroker you would need to deposit the full £1000 with the broker. A spread betting company will typically allow you to deposit a smaller "margin" payment of let's say 20%. So in this case you can make the equivalent of a £1000 investment by depositing only £200 with the spread betting company. But beware! In the absence of a stop order, you are still risking a full £1000, and the spread betting company will come knocking for the balance of £800 (it's called a "margin call") if your chosen stock goes bust. This is important, and one of the reasons that traditional investors don't like leverage.

Leverage simply means that the spread betting company takes a smaller deposit than it actually needs to cover your full risk, and it lends you the rest of the money. It's the same as when a bank or building society lets you purchase a £100,000 house with only a 20% deposit, and – just like the bank - the spread betting company will charge you interest for lending you the rest of the money.

The upside of leverage is that if the stock underlying your £1000 equivalent bet rises by 20% (lucky you) then you made not 20% profit but 100% profit on your deposit... because you only deposited £200 to cover your risk in the first place. The downside of leverage is that if the stock underlying your £1000 equivalent bet falls by 20% then your £200 deposit is totally wiped out!

Leverage has a good side and a dark side, a yin and a yang, but with the right risk-management mechanisms in place it is possible to learn to love leverage.

Overnight Financing and Rolling Charges

In exchange for providing the leverage on a smaller margin payment, the spread betting company will charge you interest in the form of overnight financing or rolling charges. On daily rolling bets, which may also be called Daily Funded Bets (DFB) or Daily Funded Trades (DFT), your account will be debited each evening by an amount equivalent to the London Interbank Offered Rate (LIBOR) plus a fixed percentage... divided by 365. With LIBOR at a low 1%, the interest rate you are charged maybe LIBOR + 2% = 3%. While the "rate" will be the same regardless of your bet size, the absolute amount will be proportional to your bet size.

If the overnight financing on your £1-per-point spread bet costs £0.01-per-day, a double-size £2-per-bet on the same stock or other financial instrument would cost you £0.02-per-day to keep open.

Just like when you invest in a buy-to-let property and you hope that your rental income plus capital appreciation will more-than-offset the costs of your buy-to-let mortgage, so with rolling spread bets you hope that the dividend receipts (if any) plus capital appreciation will more-than-offset the costs of the overnight rolling charges.

Say "No" to Dealing Fees and Commission

Unlike traditional share dealing, you do not pay a "dealing fee" or commission when you open or close a spread bet. Nor do you have to pay the 0.5% Stamp Duty Reserve Tax (SDRT) that is levied when you buy shares. All you pay is the difference between the buying and selling prices: the spread. Oh, and those overnight financing charges on any rolling spread bets that you hold for more than one day.

The situation is slightly different with Contracts for Difference (CFD), which are similar to spread bets and are offered by many of the same providers. You do pay commissions or "dealing fees" when opening and closing CFD positions.

Say "No" to Tax

Spread betting is often touted as "tax-free" because, as gambling rather than investing, you (currently) do not have to pay capital gains tax or income tax on your spread bet winnings. As well as providing a potential tax advantage compared with traditional share dealing, it's also one less thing to declare on your tax return.

The situation is slightly different with Contracts for Difference (CFD), which are similar to spread bets and are offered by many of the same providers. You do pay capital gains tax on CFD profits.

Her Majesty's Revenue and Customs (HMRC) in the UK is not necessarily missing a trick by not taxing spread bet "winnings", because they do tax the profits of the spread betting companies just as they tax any other gambling firm or other organisation. If the HMRC taxed spread bettors individually, not only would it be an administrative nightmare, but also they might actually take less tax by allowing you to offset your spread bet losses against your other gains. And they know that, unfortunately, most of you will be losers!

Take note that tax laws can change, and they can also be subject to individual circumstances. Although there are no known cases to my knowledge, there is a theoretical possibility that the HMRC could propose taxing you as a "professional" trader if you derive all or most of your income from spread betting. It's a grey area, but not one to get overly alarmed about since you are not even obliged to declare your spread bet winnings on your tax return.

Say "Goodbye" to Shareholder Perks

As well as saying "no" to dealing fees and tax, spread bettors also need to say "goodbye" to shareholder perks.

One of the benefits of holding shares was that some stock-holdings came with shareholder perks. Maybe you got a discount from the car rental firm whose shares you owned. Because you don't own shares when spread betting, you don't get any shareholder perks, but in these days of shares being held in nominee accounts I bet not many of you claimed your perks anyway. So you won't miss them.

Essential Similarities between Spread Betting and Share Dealing

Spread betting is different from traditional share dealing in the ways outlined above, yet it is also very similar.

Up-Shares, Down-Shares

Placing a "long" spread bet is pretty much the same as buying shares of a company. If the share price goes up then you make money, and if the share price goes down then you lose money. Whether you invest £1000 or spread bet £10-per-point on a 100p-per-share stock (which gives you exactly the same amount of risk) then...

- If the share price doubles, you've made a £1000 profit.

- If the company goes bust, you've lost £1000.

On a risk-reward basis it's exactly the same thing, except that many newbie spread bettors come unstuck because they think that they are risking only £200 (if that is the required deposit) when they place the £1000-risk bet.

Spread Betting Pays Dividends!

Many first-time spread bettors who are lured into day trading commodities or foreign exchange (Forex) currency pairs don't realise that they will receive dividend payouts on their longer-term equity and index bets just like a traditional stockholder would. The good news is that you receive the dividend adjustments in your spread betting account sooner than the regular stock-holders would; on the ex-dividend date rather than at a later payment date. The bad news is that you receive only 90% (and with some spread betting companies, 80%) of the dividend. At the time of writing SpreadEx is one of the spread betting companies that pays the higher 90% of the declared dividend.

So with some minor differences aside, spread betting pays dividends just like traditional share dealing does. Here is an example of a dividend payment – which in this case is serving to offset some of the spread bet rolling charges – as you would see it on the Capital Spreads platform:

Date/Time	Transaction	Credit/(Debit)	Balance
20.03.2012 23:46:13	Credit from Dividen...	7.92	733.15
20.03.2012 23:46:13	Debit for Rolling Tr...	(0.01)	725.23
20.03.2012 23:46:13	Debit for Rolling Tr...	(0.01)	725.24
20.03.2012 23:46:13	Debit for Rolling Tr...	(0.01)	725.25

Rival spread betting company IG Index provides a handy report, which details how the costs (in rolling charges) and dividend receipts have stacked up during the life of each trade.

Spread Betting vs. Share Dealing Cost Comparison

For an article I wrote some time ago I devised a spreadsheet to compare the costs of holding a spread bet position rather than a traditional share holding over various time periods and in various interest rate environments. With a particular set of assumptions - which I'll discuss shortly - the spreadsheet looks like this:

It shows that for an investment (or equivalent spread bet size) of £10,000 or less held for a period 30 days or less, it is more cost-effective to hold the spread bet rather than the traditional investment - because the spread bet financing charges amount to less than the share dealing fees. For a small bet equivalent to a £100 "investment", spread betting is more cost-effective than share dealing for as long as five years. These cases where "Spread Betting Wins" are shown in green (if you're reading in colour).

Note that for a bigger investment of say £10,000 or more, held over three months or more, traditional share dealing becomes more cost-effective. However, if you have exactly £10,000 to "invest" then from a risk perspective you should consider spreading (no pun intended) the investment across ten separate £1,000 positions, in which case spread betting once again becomes more cost-effective.

Cost Comparison Assumptions

In devising the cost comparison spreadsheet I made several assumptions as follows:

- Base interest rate (LIBOR) at 1%.

- Spread betting company financing additional charge at 2.5%.

- Extra bid-ask spread on spread bet markets vs. stockbroker offered shares of 0.2%.

- Stamp Duty Reserve Tax (SDRT) on share purchases of 0.5%.

- Share dealing fee on both purchase and sale of £10.

Well, interest rates change, and spread betting companies and stockbrokers change their fees. If we plug in a different set of assumptions we get a subtly different result, but the overall conclusion remains the same - that spread betting is more cost-effective than traditional share dealing when making smaller (or more diversified) "investments" over shorter timescales.

Share Dealing Fee	£ 7.50	LIBOR	5.00%	SB Financing	3.00%	SB Extra Spread	0.50%	Stamp Duty	0.50%
Position Size (across)	£ 10.00	£ 100.00	£ 500.00	£ 1,000.00	£ 2,000.00	£ 5,000.00	£ 10,000.00		
								<-Share	
Holding Period (down, in days)	£ 15.05	£ 15.50	£ 17.50	£ 20.00	£ 25.00	£ 40.00	£ 65.00	Dealing Costs	Colour key
7	-£ 14.99	-£ 14.85	-£ 14.23	-£ 13.47	-£ 11.93	-£ 7.33	£ 0.34	1 week	Spread Betting Wins
30	-£ 14.93	-£ 14.34	-£ 11.71	-£ 8.42	-£ 1.85	£ 17.85	£ 50.75	1 month	Share Dealing Wins
90	-£ 14.80	-£ 13.03	-£ 5.14	£ 4.73	£ 24.45	£ 83.63	£ 182.26	3 months	
180	-£ 14.61	-£ 11.05	£ 4.73	£ 24.45	£ 63.90	£ 182.26	£ 379.52	6 months	
365	-£ 14.20	-£ 7.00	£ 25.00	£ 65.00	£ 145.00	£ 385.00	£ 795.00	1 year	
730	-£ 13.40	£ 1.00	£ 65.00	£ 145.00	£ 305.00	£ 785.00	£ 1,585.00	2 years	
1825	-£ 11.00	£ 26.00	£ 185.00	£ 385.00	£ 785.00	£ 1,985.00	£ 3,985.00	5 years	

The Long and Short of Financial Spread Betting

Much of the coverage in this book will, for simplicity, be presented on the basis that you will be trading "long": buying a spread bet in the expectation of a price rise and then selling the bet (to close it) at a profit when the price has risen.

Unlike traditional share dealing, it is perfectly possible to do the opposite by going "short": selling a spread bet in the expectation of a price fall and then buying back the bet (to close it) at a profit when the price has fallen. In the following figure I have re-cast the original spread betting example that I presented in this chapter as it might have played out for a "short" trader. On the first bet, this trader wins £28 by selling short at £2-per-point before enjoying a 14-point price fall. On the second bet he loses £23 by selling short at £1-per-point and suffering a 23-point price rise (including the effect of the bid-ask spread).

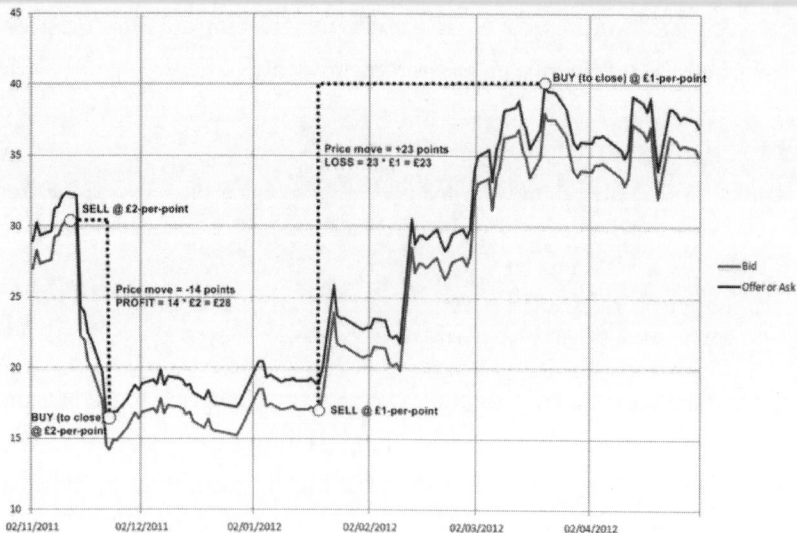

Once again this is not an example of good trading, but it shows how a spread bettor can make money by selling short prior to a price fall, or lose money by selling short prior to a price rise. The long and short of it is that spread betting is entirely agnostic regarding which way you choose to bet.

As legendary trader Jesse Livermore once said:

"There is only one side of the market and it is not the bull side or the bear side, but the right side."

The Long and Short of Rolling Charges and Dividends

Well, it's not quite true to say that spread betting is *entirely* agnostic regarding which way you choose to bet. There are a couple of subtleties regarding rolling charges and dividend receipts:

- Theoretically you should *receive* rather than *pay* overnight financing (rolling) charges on any short spread bets you hold. If base interest rates were at 5% you might expect to receive 5% - 2.5% (the spread betting company's "haircut") = 2.5% on your short spread bets. But with base interest rates at 0.5% you would find yourself still "paying" for the privilege of holding a short bet, to the tune of 0.5% - 2.5% = -2%. The minus sign in this case indicates that you are *paying* the net interest, albeit at a lower rate than the 0.5% + 2.5% = 3% that you might be paying to hold your long bets.

- Whereas on a long spread bet you stand to receive dividend credits when the underlying companies or indices declare their dividends, on short spread bets you are obliged to pay those dividends for the benefit of the traders taking the opposite (long) side of your short bets. Once again, the spread betting companies take a cut by crediting long traders with 80% of the dividend while debiting short traders 100% of the dividend – with the possible exception SpreadEx, which at the time of writing credits or debits 90% of the dividend amount.

Making Money, not Storing Wealth

Many people think that you need a lot of money in order to start spread betting, but I don't think that's true. And it may even be detrimental to have a lot of money burning a hole in your pocket during the spread betting learning curve, because: the more money you think you can afford to lose, the more money you will lose! I used to think that in order to make a lot of money in the markets, you needed to start with a lot of money. I now know this not to be true, at least as far as spread betting goes.

One of my friends once asked me "How much money do I need to have available to invest in order to start betting?"

Apart from the fact that the word "invest" in his question was probably the wrong word to use, the simple answer was... "Very little!"

Making Money

Thanks to the leveraged nature of spread betting, in two "real money" trials that I ran in 2009 I was able to turn two lots of £300 (held with two different spread betting companies) into two lots of £9,000 within six months using a position trading strategy. From £600 to £18,000 or thereabouts was a 3000% increase. This is completely at odds with the conventional wisdom that you should aim to make the same £18,000 by securing (for example) a 4.5% return on your £400,000 life savings.

Since then the markets have not been so kind to my preferred position trading strategy (other strategies have fared better), but I've managed to keep my losses to a mere fraction of those winnings by...

Not Storing Wealth

I would never deposit a £400,000 "life savings" pot into a spread betting account for safe keeping, because I know that the beneficial leverage can also become malevolent leverage.

Since my last winning streak, I have occasionally seen draw-downs of up to 50% of the funds I have deposited into spread betting accounts, which makes it all the more fortunate that I only ever re-deposit a small fraction of my previous "winnings". You don't want to lose £200,000 of your £400,000 life savings, and you probably don't even want to lose £9,000 of your £18,000 last winnings - even though the prospect of another 3000% increase to £540,000 would make it very tempting indeed!

To my mind, it's best to treat financial spread betting as a way of potentially making a lot of money from very little, with a view to then finding a safe haven (if there is such a thing) as a store of your accumulated wealth. This applies even to longer-term position trading and not just to day trading; and it looks something like this:

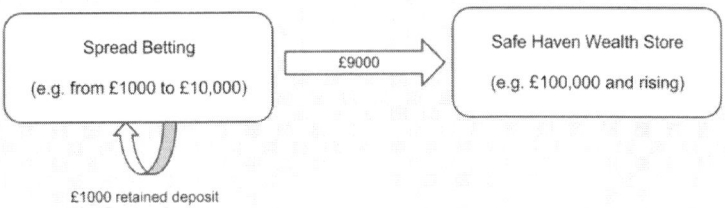

Should YOU Be Spread Betting?

Obviously I can't answer this question for you, because I don't your circumstances and I'm not authorised to give advice. My generic answer is that you should consider spread betting if...

- You want to learn the trading and investment ropes using a lot less money than you would need to "invest" with a conventional stockbroker.

- You want to try and trade small amounts of money up to large amounts of money, and you're not looking for spread betting to be a safe haven for your accumulated wealth.

- You don't want your trading profits to be degraded by paying tax (currently, in the UK) or you don't like filling in tax returns unnecessarily.

- You are willing to invest your time in learning how to manage your trading risk.

- You do not have the kind of devil-may-care attitude that will lead you to "bet the farm" on one throw of the metaphorical dice.

Can YOU Make Money Spread Betting?

Well, that's the idea, isn't it? But you'd be surprised at how many people do it despite not making any money at all.

Whether they care to admit it or not, for many people spread betting is a form of entertainment that ranks alongside bingo, horse racing and poker. But whereas bingo is a game of pure chance, horse racing and poker (and financial spread betting) imply at least some degree of skill such that there are "professionals" who make money out of it... or at least try to. Whoever heard of a "professional" bingo player?

Some people play the markets via spread betting and other forms of speculation (including "investing") because they enjoy the intellectual challenge of pitting their wits against the markets; for much the same reason that people play intellectual games like chess. Spread betting can be harmless enough as a challenging "hobby" if you confine your play to small stakes, and it's a hobby that – if you're lucky – could pay off in a way that spending your time on the golf course won't.

When all is said and done, most of us go into spread betting with the intention of making money. And some of us do. There are different ways of measuring whether you are making money by spread betting, and it depends on your trading timescale, but the acid test is this:

Have you managed to withdraw more from your spread betting account than you ever deposited? Then you've made money, and your spread betting has henceforth become a self-sufficient money machine.

Is Spread Betting Dangerous?

Some popular "investment" web sites steer their readers away from financial spread betting on the grounds that it is dangerous compared with traditional investing. But I think they're dead wrong.

I think that first-time financial speculators might benefit from trying their hands at spread betting before embarking on a journey down the traditional investment road, because:

- Spread betting allows you to get started with very small stakes, less than £1000, whereas traditional investment requires a much larger pot of cash in order to achieve meaningful diversification.

- Spread betting encourages you to hone your money - and risk - management skills by making protective stop orders (for example) both necessary and obvious.

In my opinion, if you can't make money by spread betting then you are unlikely to be able to make money as an investor.

The one caveat is the fact that spread bets are *leveraged* or *geared*, which means that you could lose (and owe the spread betting company) more than the amount you deposited with them initially; but no more than you would lose on a size-equivalent traditional investment in the same market. I'll return to this theme in a later chapter, but in simple terms:

- A £200 deposit leveraged up to £1000 via a spread bet puts the larger £1000 "at risk".

- A £1,000 investment puts exactly the same £1000 at risk for exactly the same reward.

So what's the difference?

Once you realise that in a spread betting account you are actually risking the higher leveraged amount, and that your risk is exactly the same as having invested the higher amount in the traditional way, you discover that spread betting is no more dangerous than any other form of financial speculation – including the supposedly-more-sensible "investment".

With the market mayhem of recent years, you might think that you'd have to be mad to consider spread betting or any form of financial speculation. But I see it like this:

If you can make it work (or fail not too badly) during times of market meltdown then you should be able to reap the rewards when the good times roll.

I know this is Not What You Want to Hear

Not so long ago I had a one-to-one session with a friend of a friend who wanted to get into financial spread betting. Although he was more than happy with what he paid for the "education" I provided, I could tell in his eyes and in his voice that he wanted something else, something that I didn't give him. That something was "excitement".

Ah, I remember it well - those days when I to dreamed of quitting the rat race to make millions from the comfort of my own home after having read just a few books about financial trading. How I imagined myself metaphorically shouting "buy" into one phone while simultaneously shouting "sell" into the other phone. Yes, that's what he was thinking too.

I was sorry to have to tell him, and I'm sorry to have to tell you, that it really isn't like that. It can be a hard and costly slog learning the spread betting ropes, and you can take two steps backwards for every three steps forward on the road to achieving any degree of consistency. And when you think you've got it cracked, the market will humble you once again. Or even worse, it won't, and you'll think you're the master of the universe that you always believed you were.

And yet, I have found that if you forget about the excitement and the lure of the untold riches, and concentrate on devising an approach (like my preferred position trading approach) that reduces risk (perhaps using stop orders) then one day something good might happen. It might surprise you with how big it is and how fast it happens. How exciting! But then you'll have to sit back, persist with your strategy, and be patient while you wait for it to happen again.

I know it's not what you want to hear, but it's the way it is.

Chapter Summary

In this chapter we have looked at what financial spread betting is, how it is similar to – yet different from – traditional share dealing, and how the "costs of doing business" compare over different time periods. I have suggested that leveraged spread betting may be better thought of as a way of turning a small amount of capital into a large amount of capital rather than as a vehicle for preserving existing wealth.

Is financial spread betting more dangerous than traditional investment? When viewed through a leverage-adjusted lens – I don't think so!

Before delving into the nuts and bolts of spread betting, in the next chapter we'll take a first look at the various trading styles that you might employ: from short term day trading to longer term position trading, and from fundamentals-based investing to chart-based technical trading.

2 – Trading Timescales and Styles

Before we look at opening a spread betting account and placing a first spread bet in the next chapter, it's worth reviewing (in brief) the various trading styles that you might adopt when spread betting.

I'll state at the outset that, even when spread betting, my preferred trading style is the longer-term position trading style that has something in common with traditional "investing" and which will appeal to you if you come from a traditional investment background with a traditional investment mindset. But position trading is not the only trading style, and there are other trading styles that are practised over different trading timescales.

I'll also state at the outset that despite usually taking the "long view" on spread bets, both in the directional sense of buying "long" and in the timescale sense of holding for the long term, I am more inclined to trade on the basis of technical price action than on an assessment of company fundamentals. It doesn't mean that you have to do the same, and in the remainder of this chapter I'll review your options for trading different styles over different time periods.

Day Trading

Although I do not consider myself personally to be a "day trader" as such, I did have the honour of once being mentioned as a day trader in the Money section of the UK's Sunday Times newspaper.

It's probably a fair bet (no pun intended) to assume that most first-time spread bettors will start out with the notion that they will be "day trading". It sounds so glamorous, doesn't it? And with many of the spread betting companies shouting from the rooftops about their fast execution and tight spreads, there is seemingly nothing to stop you having a go.

So do have a go, and good luck with it, but be mindful that the spread betting companies only make money – via the bid-ask spread – when you open and close positions. The more you trade in and out, the more money the spread betting companies make, but of course it's not a problem for you if you are also making money on those trades.

The other problem with day trading is that you are up against the professional full-time traders, their trading algorithms (computer programs), and – dare I say it? – their inside information. So it's difficult to compete with them if you're also trying to hold down a full-time regular job that prevents you from being glued to your computer screen all day. I do have that luxury, but I'm guessing that most of you don't.

Having set you expectations at a suitably low level, now let's look at what day trading is.

Day Trading Explained

Day trading means opening one or more trades during the day and then closing them at the end of the trading day for whatever profit (or less) has been accrued during the day. A day trade could last for just a few seconds, several minutes or even hours, but no longer than a day.

The benefits of day trading are:

- You notch up some profit (and hopefully not a loss) each and every day, so you can say "Hey, I made £100 today!"

- Because you hold no trade positions overnight, you incur no overnight financing costs and cannot be adversely affected by overnight price gaps on your trades.

The downsides of day trading are:

- You trade more often, which means you lose out more often on the bid-ask spread, but at least you don't pay an additional "dealing fee" each time you open or close a trade as you would with traditional share dealing.

- Your profit is limited to whatever profit you can accrue in a day, so you won't get any extra benefit if the FTSE 100 index (for example) goes even higher tomorrow.

Oh, and just to be clear: when day trading you don't have to wait until the end of the trading day if you want to close a trade early at a good profit.

Day Trading Example

The following chart demonstrates a successful day trade. The trader opened a long spread bet at the first signs that the price of Skyepharma shares was stirring on the morning of April 20 2012. When the UK market closed that day at 4.30pm, the trade was closed for a profit of 40 points - which equates to £40 on a £1-per-point spread bet and a more respectable (for a day's work) £400 profit on a £10-per-point spread bet.

Skypharma Chart courtesy of Google Inc. (annotated)

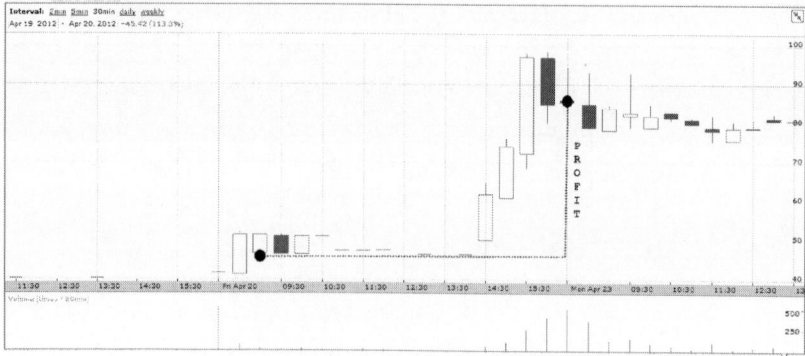

Note that this day trader could have eked out an additional 10 points of profit, i.e. 25% more profit, by closing the trade manually before the end of the trading day. However, we can deduce what he "should have done" for an even greater profit only with the benefit of our perfect hindsight.

If this day trading example has made you feel like you want to rush out and start day trading yourself, then a reality check is in order. What if the price had gone the other way, leaving you tens or hundreds of pounds down at the end of the day? You will read later how such trades must be protected, for example using a stop order.

Swing Trading

Trading over the course of a day is not the only trading timescale, and for most people it would be impractical. For those people, it may be more effective and prudent to consider placing trades that should play out over the course of a few days or even weeks. This is swing trading.

Swing Trading Explained

Swing trading is a longer-term trading style than day trading, in which the trader aims to benefit from short-to-medium-term price fluctuations when a financial instrument trades within a "trading range". In the example that follows, you will see how it is possible to capture several profits over the course of a few weeks by buying a stock (or other financial instrument) when the price approaches the bottom of a trading range and then selling it when the price approaches the top of a trading range.

Swing Trading Example

In the following chart, look at how the price of the FTSE 100 index moved up and down within a trading range while (on the grand scale) going nowhere but sideways. By repeatedly buying the FTSE 100 index at a price of 5000 and then selling at a price of 5300, the swing trader was able to bank four lots of £300 profit (assuming a £1-per-point spread bet) during the two months that the FTSE apparently "went nowhere".

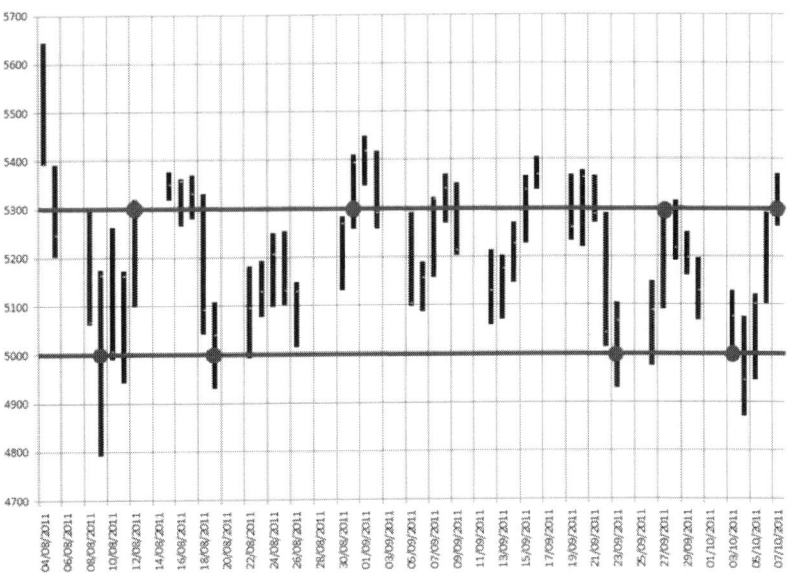

The even better news is that the trader who was willing to go short as well as long, by selling short at 5300 each time rather than merely selling out, could have banked an additional 3 x £300 on his £1-per-point spread bets. So in total there was a possible £2100 on offer here per £1-per-point bet; or – for all of you high rollers out there – a possible £21,000 for just two months work with a £10-per-point spread bet.

The downside (and there always is one) is that a £10-per-point spread bet on the FTSE 100 at 5000 would imply risking a massive £50,000 if we assumed that it was possible for the entire index to "go bust". The spread betting company would flatter you by asking for a much lower deposit in order to take the trade, but you could still be taking a big risk that is disproportionate to the amount of profit on offer... unless you were able to limit your risk absolutely using a guaranteed stop order (which we'll discuss later).

The other downside to swing trading (okay, there are two downsides rather than one) is that in all likelihood that trader could not have known in advance that the price levels of 5000 and 5300 would denote the optimal buying and selling prices. He could only really have deduced that there was a "trading range" once it had played out a while, by which time – you guessed it – it may have been too late.

Position Trading

My preferred trading style is the trading-cum-investment style known as position trading. It should be of particular interest to those coming from a traditional share dealing / investment background or those intending to operate via a spread betting account in addition to a traditional share dealing brokerage account.

Position Trading Explained

The aim when position trading is to hold a stock position (or more likely several stock positions) for as long as possible... but no longer. As the price of your chosen stock keeps rising, you keep holding, all the while raising your protective stop order in order to "lock-in" an increasing amount of profit. When the prevailing up-trend reverses – as eventually it will – the stop order closes your position (or positions) for whatever profits have accrued. While the position is in play for several weeks, months, or even years, any dividend credits that you receive will help to offset the ongoing financing charges that were outlined in Chapter 1 – Introduction to Financial Spread Betting.

Position Trading Example

The following chart illustrates a position trade that played out over the course of four months from November 2011 to April 2012. Having established a position in this stock at less than 15p-per-share, the position trader held on for as long as possible throughout the prevailing up-trend. He regularly revised his protective stop order upwards as indicated by the dotted line, until eventually the stop order triggered and closed the position automatically when the price trend reversed. This trader made a 16-point profit, which was more than his initial "risk" of 14 points and which therefore represents a 100%+ profit over four months. Because the spread betting company would have required a mere 20%-or-so "margin" deposit when opening the position, it could be argued that the return-on-investment was in fact several hundred percent! And it could have been much more if the price had risen further before the position stopped out.

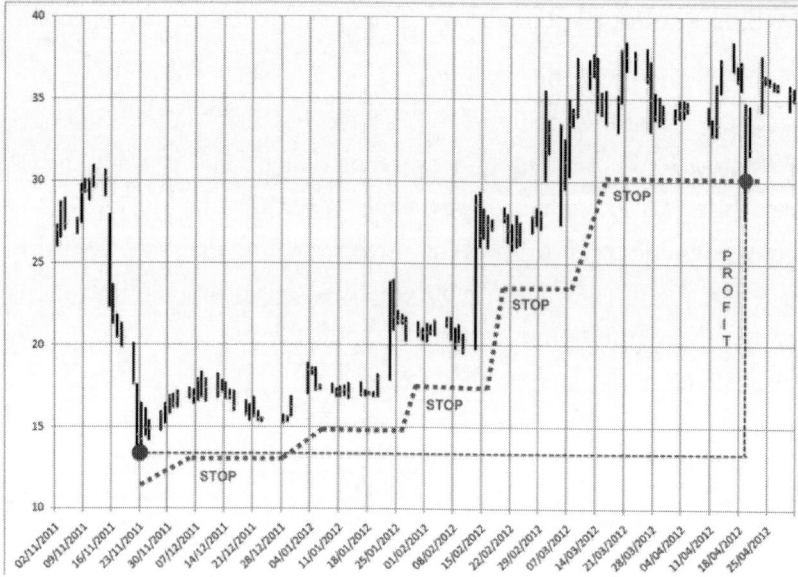

Note that in an alternative scenario, the price could have fallen rather than risen shortly after the trade was opened. The trader would then have faced a choice between holding the losing position in the hope of an eventual recovery (usually not recommended) or closing the position for a small loss – perhaps automatically thanks to the protective stop order that we'll discuss later.

Best of Both Worlds

You don't actually have to choose between a shorter-term trading style like swing trading and a longer-term trading style like position trading, because it may be possible for you to have the best of both worlds. The following chart shows how there were a number of small "swing trading" profits to be made in this particular market by buying and selling weekly at the bottom and top (respectively) of the trading range; but that a bigger prize was on offer in the form of a subsequent position trader spanning several weeks.

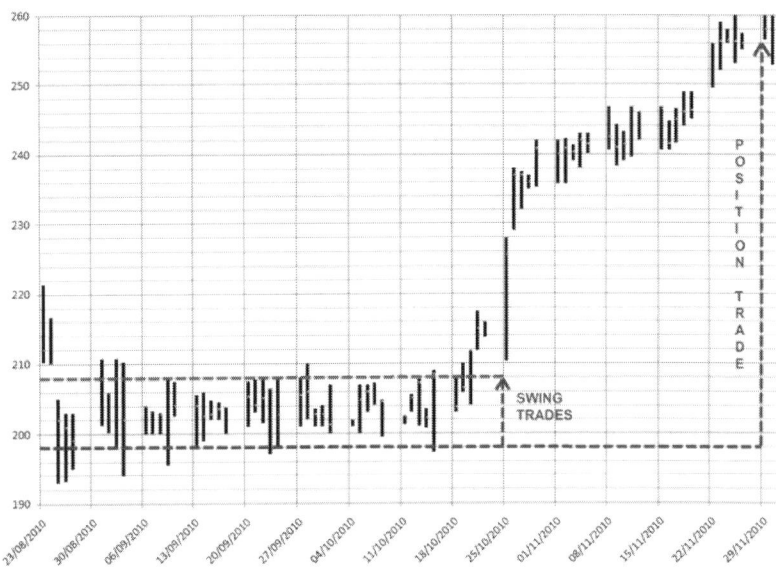

The way to get the best of both worlds in this scenario would have been to open a double (e.g. £2-per-point, or some other multiple) spread bet at the bottom of the trading range, to close out £1-per-point at the top of the trading range (while leaving a residual £1-per-point with the potential to ride higher), and then repeat by re-doubling the bet (back to £2-per-point) at the bottom of the trading range. You would capture some profit on each of the swings, and would always have a residual position with the potential to run as an ongoing £1-per-point position trade if and when the price finally broke upwards out of the trading range.

A Trading Trade-Off

Continuing from the theme of combining trading timescales, let me now contrast two trading timescales: day trading and position trading. The following chart illustrates the trade-off between time-limited day trading and time-unlimited position trading.

Chart courtesy of Capital Spreads, annotated (prices are indicative)

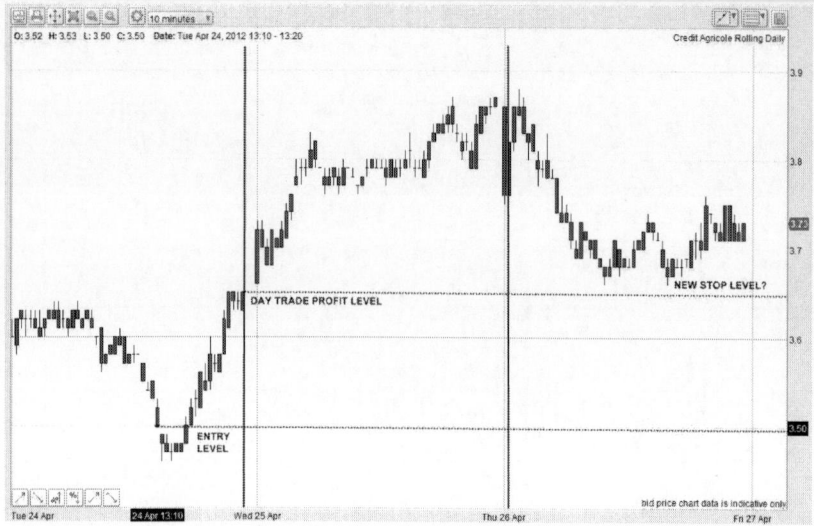

Having established a nominal £1-per-point position in Credit Agricole at a good low price of 3.51 on 24 April, by the end of the trading day a day trader would have banked a profit of about £15 (or £150 on a larger £10-per-point bet). This would have been real money "in the bank", and not bad for a day's work if we consider the larger £10-per-point stake.

By holding the position into the second day, the "peak profit" would have been more than twice as high — if the "two-day trader" had taken the initiative to close the trade at that level.

By continuing to hold the position into the third day, a longer term trader ran the risk of the price falling back (which it did) and possibly falling back below the amount that would surely have been banked by the day trader. The longer term trader would also have left themselves at continued risk of a potential overnight price-gap at any time unless a guaranteed stop order had been paid for.

A position trader would have continued to hold while raising his (or her) stop order, when convenient, to the level at which the original day trade would have closed – which, even more conveniently, coincided with a possible price support level indicated by the chart.

I can tell you that this example trade would subsequently have stopped-out at a price of 3.65. The position trader would have banked the same "gross profit" as the day trader but a lower "net profit" as a result of incurring costs of £0.06 (for financing charges on a £1-per-point bet) and £3.51 for the guaranteed stop order.

The bottom line is that in this particular "trade-off", the day trader would have banked 30% more profit than the position trader. But whereas the day trader's profit was capped, the position trader's profit could have gone so much higher.

It's a trade-off!

Fundamental Investing and Technical Trading

You may have heard about "fundamental investing", and you may even consider yourself to be a fundamental investor. You may have seen "traders" poring over charts looking for recognisable price patterns. On both counts, you might not have the faintest clue what I am talking about.

So what is fundamental investing, as distinct from technical trading, and do you really need to choose between the two?

Fundamental Investing

Fundamental investing means assessing a company's true long-term value as measured by recognised "fundamental" ratios such as the Price-Earnings (P/E) ratio. A fundamental investor hopes that the true value of the company's stock, though currently not reflected by the share price, will be reflected in the share price over time. Some fundamental investors may not be investing for capital growth at all, but rather for a steady stream of dividend income as indicated by the "fundamental" ratio known as the dividend yield.

A "fundamental" approach to trading commodities might involve assessing the prospective future supply and demand characteristics of the particular commodity that might cause the price to rise or fall.

In all cases, the fundamental investor or trader distinguishes price from value. Just because a stock, commodity, index or other financial instrument is "cheap" in the sense of its price being much lower than it used to be, this doesn't mean that it is "good value". As an analogy: the steak that is half price in the supermarket today may be cheap, but it not necessarily good value if it can only get cheaper because the sell-by date is fast approaching.

Technical Trading

Technical traders believe that everything is reflected in the price, and that ultimately something is only worth what someone else is willing to pay for it today. While this implies that prediction based on an assessment of a company's true value is futile, it doesn't mean that price movements – which are a prerequisite for making money – cannot be predicted.

For technical traders, the prediction of future price movements is based on observation of past price movements. Technical traders believe that human psychology and even computer algorithm psychology (if we can imagine such a thing) is such that historic price patterns will likely repeat themselves. If a price has rebounded upwards from a particular support price or has rebounded downwards from a particular resistance price then it will likely do so again. If the price is rising now then it will likely continue rising, and if it is falling now then it will likely continue falling.

Technical traders base their trading decisions on price charts and chart patterns.

Techno-fundamentalism

Although fundamental investing and technical trading are often portrayed as mutually exclusive, I don't see it that way. In a position trading strategy it is perfectly possible to make a trading decision based on the short-term price behaviour of a stock that has long-term fundamental potential.

In his book How I Made $2 Million in the Stock Market, legendary dancer-turned-speculator Nicolas Darvas recounts the story of how he migrated from being a fundamental investor to being a technical trader, ultimately to settle on the hybrid style of a techno-fundamentalist.

Note that if you're day trading, and possibly if you're swing trading too, you will be a technical trader who cares little or nothing for the "fundamental" attractions of the markets you are trading.

Choose Your Markets

When looking for spread bet markets to trade, one of the first things you'll notice is that they come in roughly two flavours:

- "Future" spread bets such as "Aviva September" or "High Grade Copper July" that have a defined expiry date and which incur no ongoing finance charges because these charges have already been factored into the length of time that the spread bet is expected to run.

- "Rolling" spread bets which may also be called Daily Funded Trades (DFT) or Daily Funded Bets (DFB) that have no fixed expiry date and which incur ongoing financing or "rolling" charts for every day that they are left open.

While daily rolling bets may be aimed at short-term traders who will hold those bets for only a few days (or only one day), and futures-style bets may be aimed at longer-term traders who expect their bets to run for up to three months, as a predominantly longer-term position trader I personally prefer the rolling bets. For me it is a simple transparent proposition that I pay financing for exactly the length of time that I keep the bet open, no more and no less. In any case, when first placing a bet I often have no idea whether it will run for a few hours or several months.

Equities

I'm a big fan of trading individual equities in a spread betting account, for a number of reasons:

- I understand individual companies and what they do.

- It is more cost effective for me to trade in and out of individual equities in a spread betting account than in a traditional stockbroker share dealing account.

- Individual equities generally have two- or three-digit prices; which means that I can take on minimal risk at £1-per-point and therefore diversify across a large number of separate positions.

- Any one of my individual equity holdings has the potential to become a ten-bagger whereas a stock index position (for example) is unlikely ever to appreciate by a factor of ten.

Perhaps the best reason for spread betting individual equities is the fact that the spread betting companies seem to want to steer us away from it. Have you ever noticed that when the spread betting companies offer some kind of sign-up bonus or other incentive, there is often a clause in the offer stating that "equity trades are excluded from this promotion"? To my mind, if someone is trying to dissuade you from doing something then it is probably a very good reason to be doing it!

At the time of writing, the widest range of national and international individual equities seems to be offered by IG Index closely followed by *London Capital Group* brands such as Capital Spreads and InterTrader.

Stock Indices

Spread betting makes it easy to bet on the rise and fall of domestic and international stock indices in a way that is not so easy (or transparent) when operating via a traditional stock brokerage share dealing account. You can bet on the rise and fall of the FTSE 100 and FTSE 250 indices, and you can bet on whether you think the German DAX and French CAC stock markets will rise or fall, not to mention being able to place bets on the American and other international stock indices.

Note that these markets may have different names from the names of the stock indices that you are used to, but it should be easy enough for you to figure out which indices are represented by the markets labelled UK 100 Rolling Daily and Wall Street Rolling Daily.

Unlike an index tracking fund or Exchange Traded Fund (ETF) held in a traditional brokerage account, an index spread bet is entirely transparent in the way that a rise or fall generates a profit or loss – with no such thing as a "tracking error". It is also just as easy to "go short" by betting on a stock index falling as it is to "go long" by betting on a stock index rising.

Stock indices tend to be higher priced than individual equities, e.g. the UK 100 index at 6000 compared with the price of Vodafone shares at 170 or Dixons Retail shares at 15, which means that the potential points moves (though not percentage moves) on stock indices are likely to be much greater and more costly in monetary terms if your bets move against you. On the other hand, these trades are likely to be more profitable more quickly in monetary terms, and it may be pretty implausible for a stock index to ever "go bust" taking all of your money with it.

Currencies

Some traders favour foreign exchange (forex) currency trading over equity and index trading because the foreign exchange markets are the largest and most liquid in the world. Which means there is less likelihood of any adverse event such as a "price gap", and you can trade currencies pretty much 24/7 which may be useful if you need to trade out-of-hours while also holding down your "day job".

Most if not all of the spread betting companies allow you to trade currency pairs such as the GBP:EUR (British Pound vs. Euro) or USD:AUS (US Dollar vs. Australian Dollar), or you might decide to check out one of the dedicated foreign exchange trading outfits such as SVSFX Securities – particularly if your jurisdiction does not permit spread betting.

Commodities

I have to admit that I am not a very active trader of commodities, apart from (in recent years) taking the odd punt on shorting metals such as silver and gold. Spread betting companies typically arrange their commodity markets into three categories, which are:

- Energies such as Crude Oil and Natural Gas.

- Metals such as Gold, Silver, Copper, Platinum and Palladium.

- Soft Commodities such as Cotton, Wheat, Sugar and Orange Juice.

If you're keen on commodities then your choice of spread betting company may be important, because some of the more esoteric commodities are only available to trade on certain platforms. For example: right now I could trade Lean Hogs and Live Cattle using IG Index but not using Capital Spreads; I could trade Platinum and Palladium using ETX Capital and SpreadEx, but again not using Capital Spreads (despite it being my favourite spread betting company on many other measures).

Chapter Summary - What's Your Style?

In this chapter we've looked at the various trading timescales from ultra-short-term day trading, through swing trading, to longer-term position trading. I've introduced the ideas of trading based on company fundamentals, on technical price action, or on both as a techno-fundamentalist trader. The chapter concluded by summarising the equity, index, currency, and commodity markets that you might choose to trade.

Before we move onto the nuts-and-bolts of opening a spread betting account and placing a first spread bet, it's time for you to decide on your trading style(s) from the ones described above. Or is it? There's nothing to say that you can't try your hand at each one – in turn or in parallel – to see which style is best suited to you and your circumstances. And if you're anything like me, you might decide to run with different trading styles in different spread betting accounts that you hold with different spread betting companies.

The most important thing to remember is that your trading style is up to you. Don't let the spread betting companies bully you into assuming the "day trader" mentality just because of their tight spreads and fast execution (nice though those things are). And don't let the spread betting companies and other trading platform providers lure you into thinking that it's all about currencies and commodities – by offering bonuses to trade those – when in your heart you know that you have a better grasp of understanding individual equities (i.e. stocks and shares).

3 – Opening an Account and Placing a Bet

This is what you've been waiting patiently for while reading through the first two chapters. Theory is all very well, but there comes a time when you need to turn theory into practice by actually opening a spread betting account and placing a bet. In this chapter we'll do exactly that. We'll place a first sample bet so that in the later (more advanced) chapters you'll have a mental picture of what I'm talking about when I use terms like "trading ticket".

Which Spread Betting Company?

As a trading author I am often asked which spread betting company I would recommend. In the ever-evolving world of spread betting there is no one-size-fits-all answer to this question, but I do have some views on the subject which might help you to choose the most suitable spread betting company for you. And it's worth pointing out at the outset that you don't have to pick just one. Try a few before settling on the spread betting company that you like, and maybe even keep a few (not too many) of your favourite accounts active – each for its own special purpose.

My favourite spread betting brands are Capital Spreads and the other brands operated by the *London Capital Group* including InterTrader and Financial Spreads.

These brands offer a wide range of individual equity markets, they provide a very user-friendly and intuitive trading platform, and they have the best guaranteed stop orders support that I have found – which can even be applied retrospectively on already-open positions.

My next favourite would be IG Index, which offers the widest range of individual equity markets that I have seen anywhere and which is one of the few spread betting companies (the other being ETX Capital) that provides a trade-through-charts facility including the ability to visualise your open trades on charts. IG Index also has a nice mobile trading app and support for optional guaranteed stop orders.

As a longer-term position trading spread bettor, the possibility of collecting dividends on equity and index positions is important to me. At the time of writing SpreadEx promises to pay out 90% of each dividend compared with the 80%-of-dividend credit offered by most other spread betting companies.

While the majority of spread betting companies encourage you to trade via their web sites or mobile apps (for iPhone and Android), some of them provide the additional option of trading via a more feature-rich application that you download to your PC. An example of this is the Saturn Trader PC platform provided by Spread Co.

One of the other popular spread betting companies is City Index, which also runs under "white label" partnership brands including Barclays Financial Spread Trading, Finspreads and Selftrade. Although I experienced some "connectivity" issues with the City Index platform(s) a few years ago, and I wasn't too keen on their daily resetting of the profit clock on open bets plus the tendency for new bets to be "referred to a trader", I have noticed improvements in all of these areas. The web interface is attractive and intuitive for new spread bettors, and some of the partner brands will be very recognizable and reassuring.

There are several other spread betting companies from which you can choose including GFT, Cantor Index, Gekko Global Markets and CMC Markets.

It's very much a "horses for courses" choice depending on whether you want a wide range of markets, low financing charges, a good mobile trading app, or higher dividend payouts; or the things that they all seem to boast, which are fast execution and tight spreads.

The Times They Are a-Changin'

Spread betting companies refresh their product offerings and trading platforms periodically, so if you've been using the same platform for a while it may be worth taking a look at what the other companies are offering which they didn't used to. At the time of writing, SpreadEx, Spread Co and Gekko Global Markets are both about to launch new trading platforms, and IG Index is updating its charting and stock analysis tools.

It has to be said, though, that when it comes to the other spread betting companies who are not updating their offerings *right now* (whenever you read this) the following may be true: if their platform ain't broke, they don't need to fix it.

Even when the spread betting companies stick with their tried-and-tested trading platform for sometime without a major "upgrade", you will find that new facilities are added on a periodic basis. Within the last year or so, Capital Spreads and some of its platform siblings like InterTrader have introduced guaranteed stop orders and trailing stop orders that previously were not supported.

You can access my list of spread betting companies and read my latest opinions of them at:

www.betterspreadbetting.com/p/companies.html

A Poor Workman Shouldn't Blame His Tools

In the real-life real-money trading run that I described in my position trading book, the one in which I generated a 3000% return within six months albeit using small stakes, I replicated the feat simultaneously in two different spread betting accounts; which were:

- A now-defunct E*TRADE Financial spread betting account running on the London Capital Group trading platform (like Capital Spreads and InterTrader) which at the time I liked very much.

- A Barclays Financial Spread Betting account running on the City Index trading platform, which at the time I did not like at all – yet I still achieved the same return.

My point is that while some trading strategies will work better on some trading platforms, choosing the best spread betting company is no substitute for choosing the most effective strategy. As an analogy: I'm sure that a great golfer like Tiger Woods would play better golf with a very poor set of golf clubs than would the guy who had "all the gear but no idea".

Where to Spread Bet Obscure Equities

My own bias is towards spread betting individual equities rather than stock indices, commodities or currencies. As such, in March 2012 I conducted a cursory survey of which spread betting companies provided the best range of individual equity markets.

Discounting the now-defunct World Spreads which would have scored highly (but not the highest) on this criterion, the results were as follows.

Equity	IG Index	Capital Spreads	City Index	Cantor Capital
Active Capital Trust	YES			
AEA Technology	YES			
ARK Therapeutics	YES		Maybe	
Assura Group	YES	YES	Maybe	
Aurelian Oil & Gas	YES	YES	Maybe	
Bahamas Petroleum	YES	YES		
Cadogan Petroleum	YES		Maybe	
Camco International	YES			
Capital & Regional	YES	YES	Maybe	
Ceramic Fuels	YES		Maybe	
Clinton Cards	YES		Maybe	
Cyril Sweett Group	YES			
IQE	YES	YES	YES	
Yell Group	YES	YES	YES	
ALM Brand				
Premier Foods	YES	YES	Maybe	YES

From the limited set of equities that I tested, it became clear to me that IG Index came out on top in the obscure equity race and that Capital Spreads (plus associate brands like InterTrader and Financial Spreads) came second. Other spread betting brands were not included because I considered them not even in the running on the obscure equity criterion, but it doesn't mean that alternative spread betting brands like ETX Capital and SpreadEx are not noteworthy when other criteria are considered.

How Many Spread Betting Accounts Do You Need?

As a spread betting author it has been in my interests to run accounts with most if not all of the spread betting companies including their "white label" partner brands – so that I could compare and contrast, for your benefit and for mine.

Needless to say, this became unmanageable and possibly unnecessary when you consider the fact that many of the apparently-separate spread betting "brands" utilise the same underlying trading platform. For example: Capital Spreads, InterTrader and Financial Spreads all run on the *London Capital Group* platform. Their offerings are therefore similar, but this doesn't mean they are identical.

An entirely separate spread betting brand like IG Index, SpreadEx or Spread Co will likely have a substantially different offering and will provide an alternative trading platform in the unlikely event that the *LCG* platform becomes unavailable for a short period of time.

What I'm saying here is that while I have rationalised my own spread betting accounts down to just a few of my favourites, there are some very good reasons for maintaining say two or three of them. Partly for platform resilience (so that you always have somewhere to trade), partly to reduce counter-party risk (see Chapter 6 – Risk Doesn't Have To Be Risky), and partly because different accounts may be useful for different reasons.

My own current preference would be to use Capital Spreads whenever possible for betting on high-priced financial instruments that necessitated *guaranteed* stop orders, and to use IG Index for betting on those obscure equities that are simply not offered for trading on any other spread betting platform. I might throw either of Spread Co or SpreadEx into the mix for one of their unique features and to add a third choice of trading platform. And that's it: just three accounts, which is the minimum that I consider to be prudent but no more than I actually need.

Alternatives to Spread Betting

Before we move on to opening a spread betting account it is worth mentioning that there are alternatives to standard spread betting, which may appeal to more experienced traders or those who aspire to be. These alternatives include fixed odds binary bets of the kind offered by BetOnMarkets, and margin trading of the kind by SVSFX Securities. In jurisdictions that do not permit spread betting, specifically the United States, contracts for difference (CFD) might present a viable alternative to spread betting, and you will find CFD trading to be offered by many of the spread betting companies plus companies such as Plus500. Many of the techniques described in this book will be applicable to those alternative trading platforms, but it may be better (for now) for you to steer clear unless you already know what you are doing.

Opening a Spread Betting Account

In most if not all cases it is free to open a spread betting account, it can be done entirely on-line with (usually) no need to send documents, and you don't need to deposit any cash when opening an account unless you want to claim a deposit-dependent sign-up bonus*. You can usually start by depositing just a little cash to begin with, and that's a good thing.

There are some restrictions on who can open an account, such as the fact that you must be at least 18 years old and you must be resident in a jurisdiction in which spread betting is not prohibited – which in particular rules out the United States. When opening an account, the spread betting companies are obliged by the regulatory authorities to assess your "suitability" by asking questions about your income, assets and understanding of trading financial instruments. Providing you are solvent, with a reasonable income and some assets, and you have some understanding of trading financial instruments – e.g. you have bought or sold shares in the past – then you should not encounter too many hurdles when opening an account.

* *At the time of writing, InterTrader (for example) offers an additional trading credit of 10% of your initial deposit.*

The "Limited Risk" Option

Some spread betting companies offer new clients the option of opening a limited risk account that attaches a mandatory stop order to every trade and which provides a limited range of markets to trade. To my mind, the irony here is that I consider it to be less risky to have access to a wide range of markets rather than a limited number of stock indices.

The "Demo" Option

Almost all of the spread betting companies let you practice first by opening a demo account with them, and most of the spread betting books advise you to do so. This makes some sense if you really have no idea what spread betting is, and if you are therefore likely to make some very simple but costly "schoolboy errors" because you don't know how to operate the tools at your disposal. But don't go thinking that your "demo" experience will be anything like your subsequent real trading experience. The tools will be the same, but the emotions won't be.

A demo account might even turn out to be dangerous; if (by sheer luck) you make a million in a day and think that you will surely repeat the feat in a real-life trading account. I believe that there is something to be said for learning the ropes at the "Trading School of Hard Knocks" by operating in a real account from day 1 – albeit a very modest account. If you have £10,000 to your name, don't deposit any more than £1000 of it into your new real-life account, and then don't go risking it all – and more – on a single leveraged-up penny stock purchase.

The Best of All Worlds

Because opening a spread betting account is so simple, and the initial deposit requirements are so low, there is a good case for opening more than one spread betting account in order to benefit from the unique offerings of each one. For example: in May 2012, Capital Spreads introduced a new Economic Calendar and Market Data portal to their Trading Tools section which may be unique to their platform. Other providers will boast unique features of their own.

I have often argued in "investing" circles that even traditional investors would benefit from opening a spread betting account with at least a small deposit, if only to access the real-time charts that may be denied them on their stockbroker's own share dealing platform. You can find a list of spread betting companies in the Appendix – Spread Betting Resources.

Anatomy of a Trading Screen

When you log into your spread betting account, you will be presented with a trading screen not dissimilar to the Capital Spreads trading screen that I have reproduced below. If your spread betting provider utilises the *London Capital Group* trading platform then it will look very similar (at the time of writing) to this one. If you're using a different trading platform, much of the essential anatomy will be the same.

Screenshot courtesy of Capital Spreads

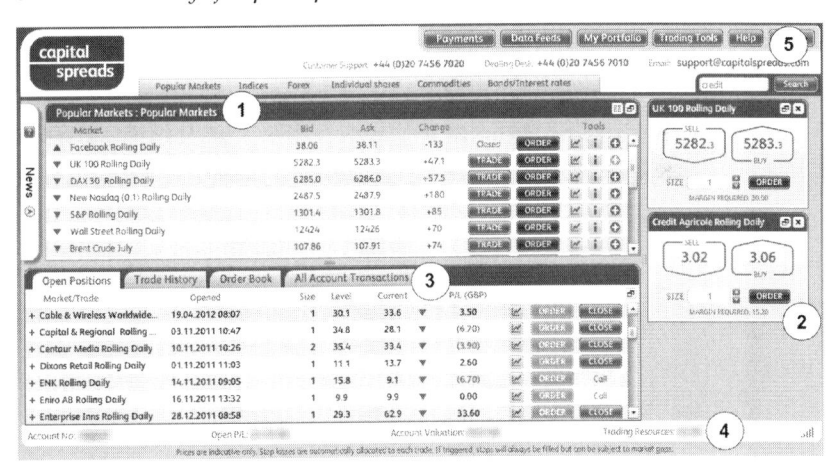

The labelled areas of the trading screen are:

53

1. Markets: Using the search box (to the right) and the various tabs for Indices, Forex etc. you can populate the markets pane with a choice of financial instruments that you might wish to trade.

2. Trading Tickets: Clicking the TRADE button for any market launches a trading ticket that allows you to place a "buy" or "sell" bet.

3. Positions and History: When you have placed some trades, your open positions will be listed with an indication of the running profit or loss as shown. Clicking the CLOSE button allows you to close any open position. You can use the other tabs in this area to see your Trade History, your future Order Book (don't worry about this for now) and your balance-affecting All Account Transactions.

4. Account Summary: A summary of your account, and in particular how much trading firepower you have left in the form of your Trading Resources is shown at the bottom of the screen.

5. Extra Functions: Additional functions, for example to deposit or withdraw cash using the Payments button, are presented at the top of the screen.

My intention here has been to give you an idea of how a typical spread betting trading screen is laid out with areas for researching markets, placing trades via trading tickets, and seeing your open positions and overall account standing. The exact layout will likely change over time from what I have shown here, and other trading platforms will differ slightly, but I expect the example trading screen layout to remain roughly right for some time.

A Note about Trading Resources

The displayed *Trading Resources* figure – which may go under different names such as *Available to Deal* or *Trade Funds Available* –

represents the amount of free cash you have available for committing to new bets.

On some spread betting platforms, notably Capital Spreads, this figure won't change except in response to balance-affecting transactions like financing charges, dividend receipts, or profits from newly-closed positions. So you need not worry too much about maintaining a minimum balance that at least covers your anticipated *rolling charges*.

On some spread betting platforms, for example IG Index and ETX Capital, your available funds may rise or fall as a function of how the prices of your open positions are rising and falling. This can be both bad (because you might stray into a negative trading funds balance) and good (because better performance leads to more available funds). On these platforms you need to keep a closer eye on your trading funds balance so that it stays above zero.

A First Spread Bet

Once you've opened a spread betting account with one (or more) of the spread betting companies, it's time to place a first spread bet. In the example that follows, I'll give a rationale for the bet and then we'll place the bet via a trading ticket.

Rationale for the Bet

On the morning of 7 May 2012, the day after socialist Francois Hollande was declared the new president of France, the price of French bank Credit Agricole's shares "gapped-down" but then appeared to have bottomed-out and begun a new upward trajectory as shown here:

Credit Agricole chart courtesy of Google Inc.

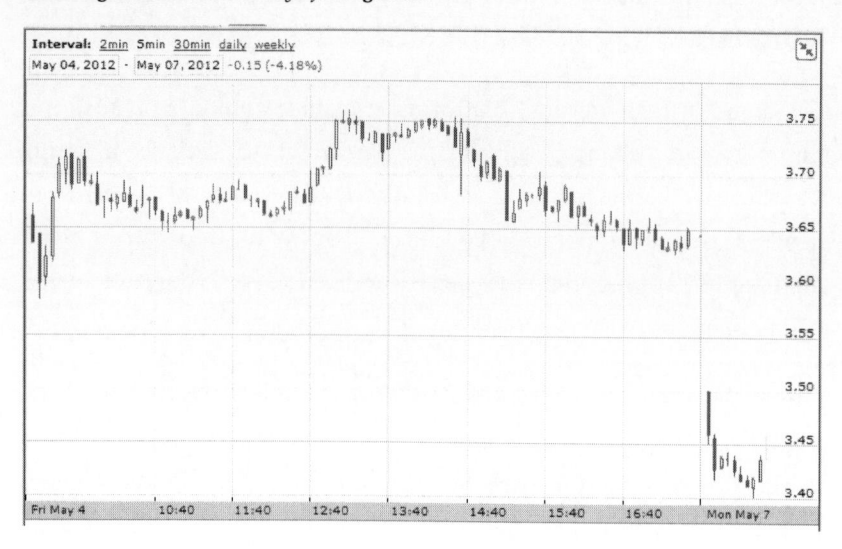

At this point you may have seen an opportunity to make a quick day trade profit of 20 points (times the number of £££s-per-point that you would bet) if the price gap "closed" from a possible entry price of 3.45 to the previous trading day's closing value of 3.65. Alternatively, you may have noticed on the longer-term price chart (see below) the fact that the price was now at or around a resistance level that possibly marked the bottom of a trading range and from which you might be able to benefit from a swing trade.

Credit Agricole chart courtesy of Google Inc.

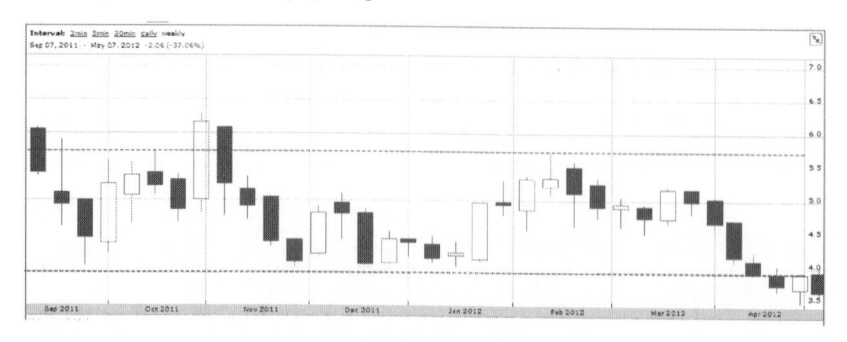

Don't worry if some of the terminology is a little unfamiliar at this point, as it will be defined more formally later. Also don't worry about whether or not this first spread bet worked out, or if your own real-life first spread bet works out. The important thing is that we have some kind of plausible rationale for placing a bet that demonstrates the process.

Placing the Bet via the Trading Ticket

After searching or browsing for the Credit Agricole Rolling Daily market in the list of available markets on your chosen spread betting platform, you would typically press the TRADE or BUY button so as to launch the trading ticket and place the bet. Note that on some platforms the open-ended daily rolling bets that I prefer may be indicated as Daily Funded Bets (DFB) or Daily Funded Trades (DFT), but the important thing is that at this stage we are not choosing a future-dated market like (for example) Credit Agricole June 2012.

Here is an example trading ticket inspired by the ones provided by Capital Spreads. It shows that I can "go long" by buying Credit Agricole at a price of 3.45 or "go short" by selling at a price of 3.41. I will go long for £1-per-point at 3.45 by pressing the BUY button, but not before entering the STOP and LIMIT values shown.

Trading Ticket courtesy of Capital Spreads (prices are for demonstration only)

Credit Agricole Rolling Daily

SELL: 3.41
BUY: 3.45
SIZE: 1
ORDER
MARGIN REQUIRED: 15.23
STOP: 10 — Points away (min: 6)
LIMIT: 200 — Points away (min: 1)
☐ GUARANTEED
☐ TRAILING

In this example you can see that I have tried for the longer-term "swing trade" by adding a contingent LIMIT that will close the bet automatically for a profit of 200 points when (or if) the price reaches 5.45. It would be a 200 point profit and not a 2 point profit in this case because on this particular market the decimals are counted as individual points or pips, so it's like betting on an equity priced at 345 rather than 3.45.

You can also see that on this trading ticket I have added a contingent STOP (or stop order) that will close the bet automatically and therefore cap my potential loss at just 10 points (or £10 on a £1-per-point bet) if the bet goes against me and the price falls from my entry price of 3.45 to a price of 3.35. On this first example trade I have risked £10 for a possible pay-off of some £200, which is an excellent risk-reward ratio.

On all spread bets it is vitally important to limit your potential loss using a stop order. On your first spread bet it is vitality important to further reduce your risk by betting at just £1-per-point or whatever minimum stake size is mandated by the spread betting platform.

Reviewing Your Open Bets

Once you have placed your first spread bet you will see it listed in your Open Positions list something like this:

Market	Level	Current	£P&L
Credit Agricole Rolling Daily	3.45	3.41	(3.00)

Any new bet that you place will show a loss initially, as a result of the difference between the buying and selling prices: the bid-ask spread. For this reason it's not usually a good idea to close a bet that you only just opened unless you are doing so to correct a mistake.

The First Winning "Day Trade"

The example bet just described was a real bet that was placed using real money, albeit as a demonstrative example.

The good news is that at close-of-play on the day that the bet was opened it was showing a profit of £10, which is the profit that the day trader would have banked when the bet was necessarily closed at the end of the trading day. The even better news (for the day trader) is that the banked "day trade" profit disappeared in the course of the subsequent couple of days; so in this case it was "one-nil" to the day trader.

While a £10 profit on a first bet of minimal risk is not a bad result, and is certainly not a loss, we need to do better than winning £10 whenever we risk £10.

4 – Tools of the Trade

In the previous chapter you have already seen some of the "tools of the trade" in the form of the trading screen and trading tickets provided by one of the spread betting companies. In this chapter we'll take a more in-depth look at the tools provided by the spread betting companies themselves and elsewhere on free-to-use web sites. Think of the "tools" as the various controls and indicators that help you to drive your car.

Stop Orders

In my opinion, stop orders are perhaps the most important weapon in the spread bettor's armoury. Some spread betting companies automatically apply a default stop-loss order to each bet that you place, to guard against it going too far against you, but you can change the stop level to what you consider to be a more appropriate stopping-out price. Some spread betting companies do not automatically apply a stop-loss order to each trade, which makes it all the more important that you get into the habit of thinking about your exit (via a stop order) when you enter each trade.

Whereas much of the conventional literature covers stop orders as a mechanism for stopping losses – hence the term "stop-loss order" – it is worth noting that stop orders may be just as useful for locking in profits on winning positions as they are for limiting losses on losing trades. They may even be used for entering new trades as well for exiting existing trades.

Guaranteed Stop Orders

Although stop orders aim to limit your potential loss at a particular level, there is no guarantee that the order will trigger at your intended level in the event that the price "gaps through" that price level on some unexpected adverse news. Actually, there is such a guarantee if your chosen spread betting company allows you to apply a *guaranteed stop order*.

Since guaranteed stop orders come at a cost (discussed shortly) my usual recommendation is to only use the "insurance" provided by guaranteed stop orders to insure the risks you can't afford to take.

For example: if you had placed a long bet on French bank Credit Agricole on 16 May 2012, you may have considered there to be a real possibility of the share price crashing (even more than it already had) if Greece was forced to exit the Euro. With the price at 3.00 but with the decimals counting as "points" for spread betting purposes, the potential loss on a total share price collapse was as high as £300 on a £1-per-point bet. It would be a big potential loss that you couldn't afford to take in your modest £1000 spread betting account, so you might have considered the £3.00 additional "insurance premium" of a guaranteed stop order to be well worth the money for the protection it afforded.

On the other hand: on your £1-per-per-point exploratory position in Dixons Retail priced at just 12-p-per-share, no stop order at all (let along a guaranteed one) would be necessary in order to protect you from the minimal £12 loss that you could easily absorb.

Retrospective Guaranteed Stop Orders

On many spread betting platforms you have to decide whether or not you want to apply a guaranteed stop order *at the time you place your bet* and it's too late to apply a guarantee retrospectively once your trade is open. The good news is that, at the time of writing, the *London Capital Group* spread betting brands such as Capital Spreads and InterTrader do allow you to guarantee your existing stop order retrospectively... albeit at an increased stop distance compared with your regular stop order.

As a concrete example I can tell you that on 14 June 2012 I opened a long spread bet on Supergroup at a price of 270.9 with a non-guaranteed stop order at 260. By 19 June the price of Supergroup shares had risen sufficiently for me to trail my stop order to just better than break-even at 272, and at the same time to guarantee the stop order (retrospectively) for an additional charge of £2.71. In a nutshell: in my Capital Spreads or InterTrader account I didn't have to pay for my guaranteed stop order until I could place it at the level I wanted it. By the following evening, the price had increased sufficiently for me to trail my newly-guaranteed stop order to 291 if I so chose. As a picture, the trade I just described looks like this:

Supergroup chart courtesy of Yahoo! Finance

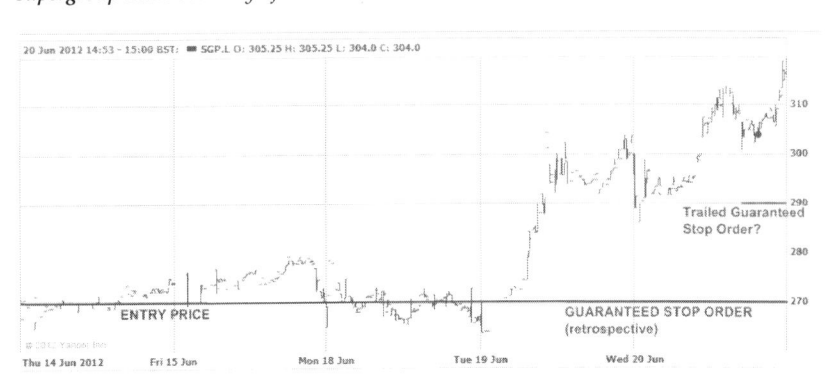

The Costs of Guaranteed Stops

Since the spread betting company is taking the risk of the price falling through your *guaranteed* stop order level, it quite rightly expects you to pay for the privilege of this "insurance" against an unexpected loss. The cost of the guaranteed stop order can take several forms:

- A one-off fee that is debited from your account balance, such as the £0.79 fee that Capital Spreads just debited (at the time of writing) in exchange for me guaranteeing a stop order on my £1-per-point Homeserve position at a level of 155.7. Considering that this spread bet would lose me more than £150 if the company went bust overnight, the 79p cost of insuring the position may be a small price to pay.

- A extra-wide spread when opening the trade, such as the additional 1.47 points that (at the time of writing) IG Index wants to add into their bid-ask spread of 162.99 - 164.11 on a any new Homeserve bet that I care to make.

- A wider stop distance that increases your risk-to-stop loss and which lessons the chance of the spread betting company needing to honour the guarantee. At the time of writing, Capital Spreads requires a guaranteed stop order to be 9.3 points rather than the non-guaranteed 2.6 points away from the prevailing price of Homeserve shares. IG Index requires the same guaranteed stop order to be 10% (about 16 points) away from the prevailing price compared with just 0.01 point away for a non-guaranteed stop order.

Note that while the first two charges are levied at the time you open the bet or guarantee the stop order, the greater distance-to-stop will not cost you at all if the price does not subsequently fall to the stop level, and it might actually help you not to set your stop orders too tight. On the other hand, if the price falls to your guaranteed stop level soon after your bet is opened, the failed trade will have cost you between £6 and £16 more (on a £1-per-point bet) than if a closer non-guaranteed stop order had been in place.

Trailing Stop Orders

Your stop orders need not be static, and it is good practice to "lock in" some of your accrued profit when a spread bet moves in your favour. The golden rule here is to always move the stop level up on a long trade and down on short trade, so as to always *reduce your risk*. Rarely if ever should you be tempted to increase your risk by moving your stop level further away from the prevailing price.

You saw an example of a trailing stop order in action in Chapter 2 – Trading Timescales and Styles, and here it is again to save you flicking back to find it:

Below, you can see how I have opened the IG Index trading ticket for an existing open bet, with a view to trailing the guaranteed stop order as close as it will go to my break-even entry price. I attempted this feat purposely outside of trading hours to demonstrate the fact that all spread betting companies (not just IG Index) prevent you from moving your *guaranteed* stop orders – on which they are taking the risk – when the markets are closed. Had I attempted this change during market hours, or on a non-guaranteed stop order, I would not have received the warning that *"You cannot move this Stop Level closer to the market level at this time".*

Example Ticket courtesy of IG Index

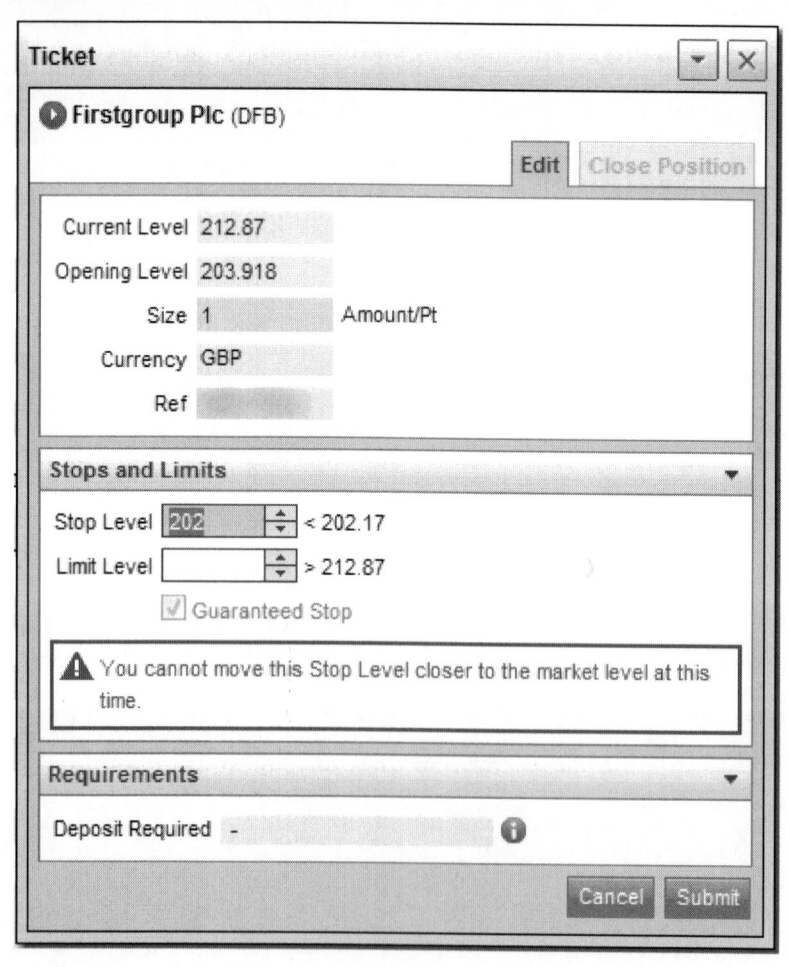

To save you the hassle of constantly monitoring your stop levels and trailing them manually, some of the spread betting companies including Capital Spreads, InterTrader, ETX Capital and IG Index allow you to indicate a stop order as a *trailing stop* that move upwards automatically at a set distance in line with the rising price (for a long bet) or downwards in line with the falling price (for a short bet).

In the ETX Capital partial trading ticket shown below, you can see how I have marked my stop order to trail the rising price of Beazley Group shares whenever the price moves by 10 points.

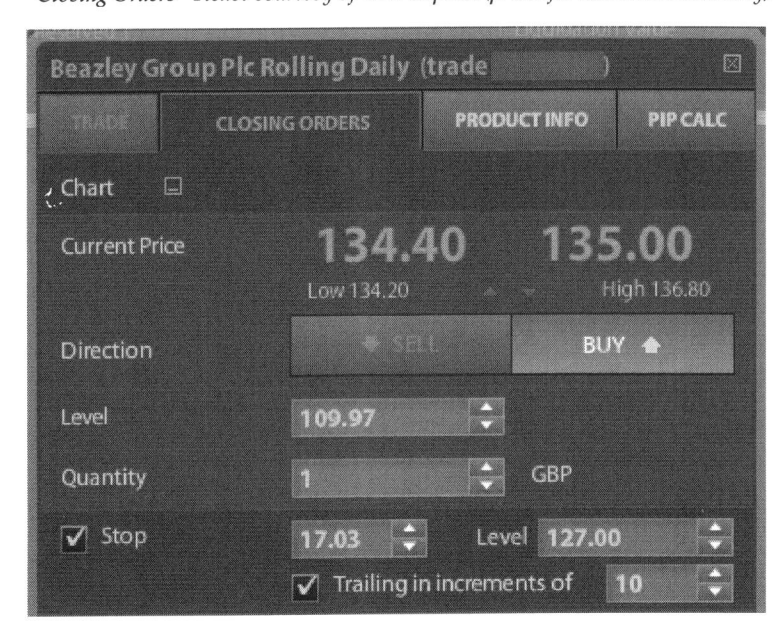

"Closing Orders" Ticket courtesy of ETX Capital (prices for demonstration only)

Less Risk Means More Trading Funds

One of the unexpected (for new spread bettors) effects of trailing a stop order is that on many spread betting platforms your available *trading funds* will increase as you reduce your risk. Try it for yourself by noting your available funds, then opening a new position with a stop order at distance of (for example) 20 points, then move the stop order ten points closer to the prevailing price, and then check your available funds again. It works slightly differently on different platforms, and it may depend on whether your position is already showing a profit or a loss, but it can be an effective way of rustling up some additional trading funds in an emergency when you think that your cupboard of available funds is bare.

Opening Orders

If you are, or intend to become, one of those spread bettors who sits in front of your trading screen(s) all day looking for opportunities to place a trade manually when the time is right then you can rely on the spread betting platforms' trading tickets. If you are more laid back — okay, let's admit it, employed in your day job — so that you can only review your potential trades each evening (or at the weekend) then you will need to utilise *opening orders* that get you into a long or short position automatically when the price hits a particular level.

An opening order ticket such as the Capital Spreads New Order ticket shown below is similar to the trading ticket we met in the previous chapter and the Closing Orders ticket shown in the previous section. Like a trading ticket, the New Order ticket is (usually*) used for opening a new position; like the Closing Orders ticket, the New Order ticket specifies a *future purchase or sale* to take place *when a particular price is reached*.

* *note that a trading ticket or an opening order may in fact close an existing trade if one already exists in the opposite direction; i.e. a short £1-per-point trade or opening order, when executed, will close an existing long £1-per-point bet that you have in play on the same market.*

Order Ticket courtesy of Capital Spreads (prices for demonstration only)

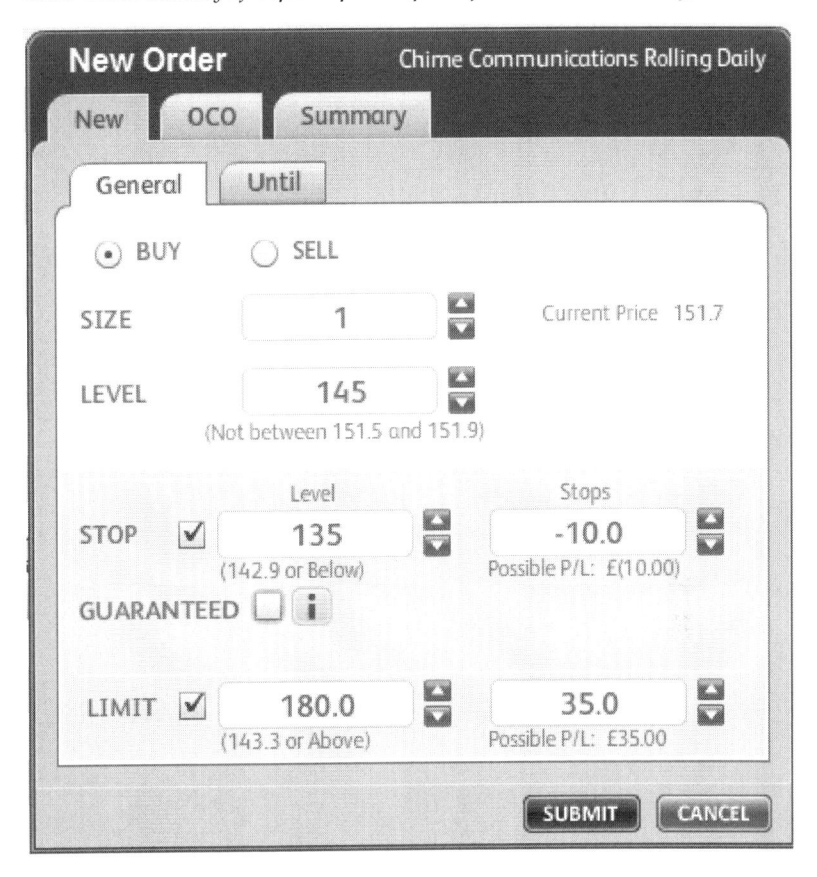

New Order — Chime Communications Rolling Daily

Tabs: New | OCO | Summary
Sub-tabs: General | Until

- ● BUY   ○ SELL
- SIZE: 1
- Current Price: 151.7
- LEVEL: 145 (Not between 151.5 and 151.9)

STOP ✓ Level: 135 (142.9 or Below) Stops: -10.0 Possible P/L: £(10.00)

GUARANTEED ☐

LIMIT ✓ 180.0 (143.3 or Above) 35.0 Possible P/L: £35.00

[SUBMIT] [CANCEL]

This New Order ticket states your intention to BUY Chime Communications automatically at £1-per-point when the price falls from the Current Price of 151.7 to a LEVEL of 145.

The lower half of the ticket becomes relevant only if and when the price falls to the required level and the order executes. The STOP and LIMIT orders are contingent orders that will be created automatically when this order executes, so that your newly-opened position will subsequently be closed at a profit (the LIMIT) or at a defined loss (the STOP).

In a nutshell: This New Order ticket will cause you to "go long" at a price of 145 and then subsequently exit for a profit of £35 (if the price rises to 180) or exit for a loss of £10 (if the price falls to 135).

Here is what an IG Index *opening order* ticket for a similar intended trade looks like at the time of writing. In this case the long position will be opened (if it is at all) at a lower price of 135.

Example Order Ticket courtesy of IG Index (prices for demonstration only)

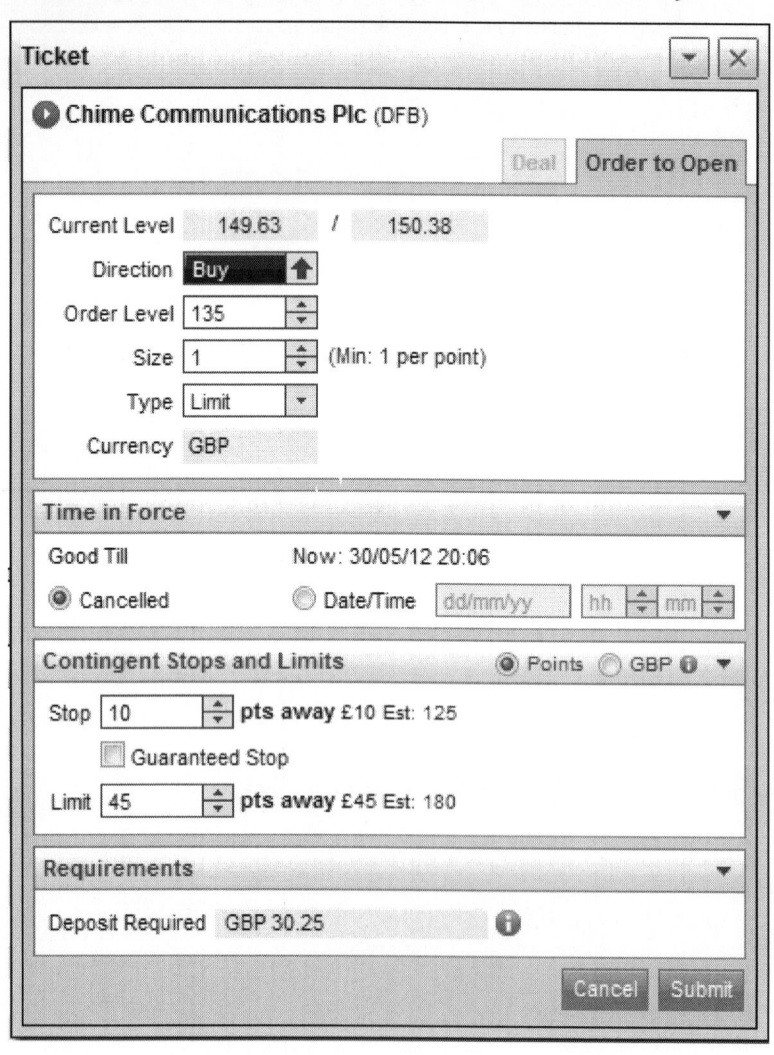

Ticket		
▶ Chime Communications Plc (DFB)		
	Deal	**Order to Open**
Current Level	149.63 / 150.38	
Direction	Buy ↑	
Order Level	135	
Size	1 (Min: 1 per point)	
Type	Limit	
Currency	GBP	

Time in Force
Good Till   Now: 30/05/12 20:06
◉ Cancelled   ○ Date/Time dd/mm/yy hh mm

Contingent Stops and Limits   ◉ Points ○ GBP
Stop 10   pts away £10 Est: 125
☐ Guaranteed Stop
Limit 45   pts away £45 Est: 180

Requirements
Deposit Required   GBP 30.25

Cancel   Submit

Note that in this case the Type of opening order is specifically indicated as Limit. This has nothing to do with the contingent Limit order detailed in the lower half of the ticket; it merely details the fact that any order to "buy" when the price falls to a specified level is a Limit order. In this context: any order to sell when the price rises is also a *limit order* whereas any order to sell when the price falls is a stop order and any order to buy when the price rises is also a stop order. Since these rules are a matter of fact rather than choice, the order type is simply deduced in the first (Capital Spreads) order ticket from your combination of direction (buy or sell) and price level.

Opening Orders are "Good Until"...

Opening orders are standing orders that are good until you cancel them, or until a specified time is reached which causes them to lapse. For example: you may which to buy into Chime Communications if the price falls to 145 (in the first example) or 135 (in the second example) providing it does so today or within a month.

The IG Index ticket includes a Time in Force section allowing you to specify that your opening order is Good Till it is Cancelled or until a particular Date/Time is reached. The earlier Capital Spreads ticket has a separate tab labelled "Until" for the same purpose.

Trading with Triggers

Suppose you want to consider placing a trade when a particular financial instrument falls to a certain price, but you simply want to be notified when this price event occurs rather than entering a trade automatically using an opening order. Some spread betting platforms provide a "triggers" facility that will notify you via email (and in some cases via SMS text message) when a particular price event occurs.

For my concrete example: let's suppose I want to be notified if ever the American S&P Index falls by 2% within any given day, which I might consider to be an overreaction. In the following Capital Spreads chart I am in the process of adding a trigger for exactly this event.

Price Chart with Trigger courtesy of Capital Spreads (prices are indicative)

This chart-driven example leads us naturally onto the subject of...

Charts

Price charts are essential for successful spread betting, and I believe this to be true whether you are practising short-term day trading, intermediate-term swing trading, or longer-term position trading.

In addition to the charts provided by the spread betting companies themselves, you will find many other paid-for and free charts provided by third parties. Personally I don't see the point in paying for charts these days when the spread betting companies provide them as a complementary (additional) and complimentary (free) adjunct to their trading platform services. Not only that, but many of the entirely free sources of financial information on the web – like Yahoo! Finance and Google Finance – provide good charting facilities, and in the case of Google Finance these have been "real-time" charts since 2012 rather than the old-style charts that suffered a 15-minute delay.

This book contains many examples of price charts, which I have attributed to the providers of those charts wherever possible.

Most if not all of the charting tools allow you to view charts over varying timescales from minutes to months, and they allow you to overlay useful technical indicators such as moving averages.

You can typically display charts in various formats including simple lines and candlesticks. Most spread bettors will use candlestick charts, so it is worth quickly reviewing how a candlestick chart should be interpreted.

In the example chart below, each "candle" represents one trading interval, which might be a day or which could be a shorter interval such as an hour or a minute. The upper and lower "wicks" of each candle indicate the HIGH and LOW prices reached during the interval, and the "body" of each candle indicates the OPEN and CLOSE prices for the period.

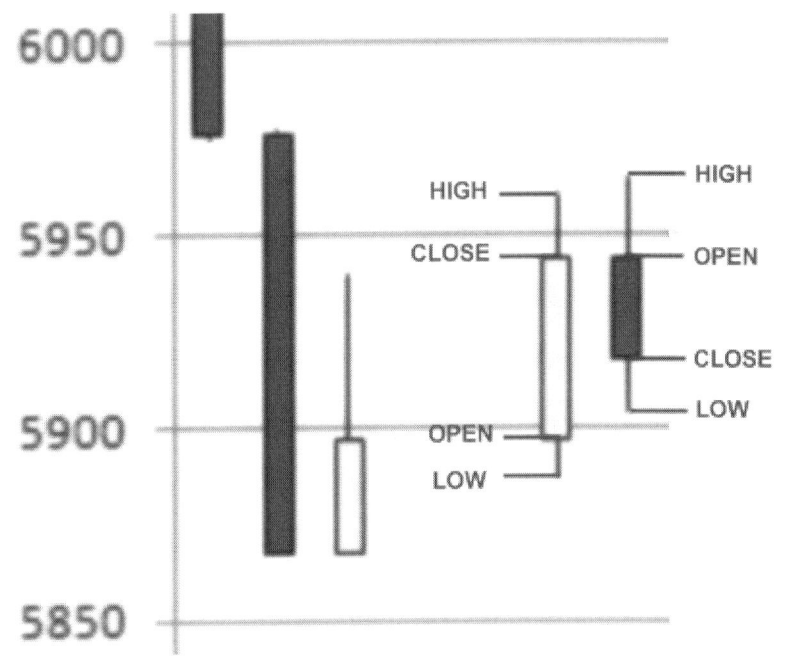

Note that when the price closes above the level at which it opened, this "bullish" condition is indicated by a hollow candle body; when the price closes below the level at which it opened, this "bearish" condition is indicated by a filled candle body.

Note also that the open price of each candle should correspond with the close price of the previous candle, unless a "price gap" has occurred.

Trade through Charts

Some spread betting companies provide a facility to "trade through charts" and to visualise your existing positions on those same charts. See how the following ETX Capital chart clearly shows that I had established a position in Enterprise Inns at a price of 29.293p-per-share, that the position moved first into loss (shaded pink) and then into profit (shaded green), and that the current market price is above the level of the stop order that I have successfully trailed to 57p-per-share.

"Trade Through" Chart courtesy of ETX Capital

In the above chart you can see that I also have the ability to buy or sell a bet on this stock, for example if I was now inclined to pyramid an additional position now that the price is falling back towards my prevailing stop order level.

ETX Capital is not the only spread betting company to offer a "trade through charts" facility. The following IG Index chart shows that I just opened a long £2-per-point FTSE 100 index position at a price of 5318.6 with a protective stop order placed 15 points below at 5303.6. I'm pleased to see (on the chart) that this spread bet has already moved into profit by £2.

"Trade Through" Chart courtesy of IG Index

As in the earlier ETX Capital example, this IG Index chart provides a mini trading ticket at the top of the chart that allows me to buy or sell this market (the FTSE 100 index) without leaving the chart.

"Trade through Charts", or "Charts on Trade Tickets"?

An alternative to allowing trades to be placed from charts is display charts on trade tickets. I have seen this alternative approach on at least stockbroker platform and on some of the spread betting mobile trading apps, and as I write this I have just received an email from Spread Co announcing that their new trading platform will include "Charts integrated within trade tickets".

Spread Betting Companies' News and Research

In May 2012 Capital Spreads introduced a new Economic Calendar and Market Data portal to their Trading Tools section, which at the time of writing can be accessed by clicking the Trading Tools tab on the Capital Spreads main page. Of course, you need to be logged into a Capital Spreads account in order to utilise the useful content provided in conjunction with the respected financial information provider Digital Look.

IG Index has a range of research and analysis tools including the INSIGHT portal which – as well as providing access to a range of market analysis tools at the time of writing – also (among many things) allows you to review your trading activity in the form of a daily, weekly, or monthly diary as shown below.

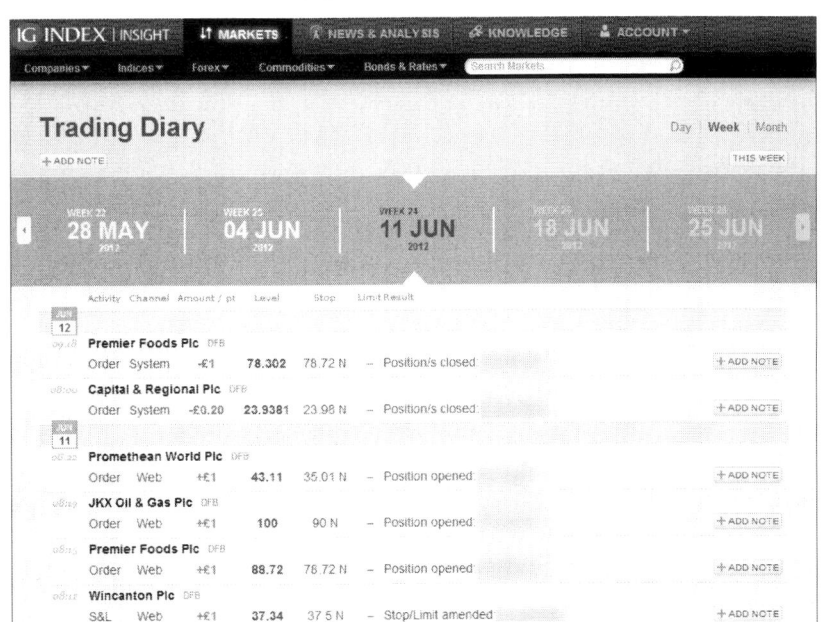

IG INSIGHT screenshot courtesy of IG Index

How cool is that?

Financial Web Sites

Besides the spread betting companies' own news and research portals, don't forget that there are many entirely free web sites offering financial news, research and commentary.

My favourite financial web sites are Yahoo! Finance and Google Finance, and for those of you who are more "investment" oriented The Motley Fool may be more appropriate.

Mobile Trading

Have you noticed the gradual shift away from traditional PC computers towards iPads and iPhones powered by the iOS operating system and tablets and smart phones powered by the Android operating system?

The spread betting companies have noticed this too, which is why most of them offer an iPhone / iPad or Android mobile trading app.

Users of Apple's iPhone and iPad are well catered for by most of the spread betting companies. Early in 2012 I reviewed the iPhone apps provided by Capital Spreads, IG Index, SpreadEx and ETX Capital for a spread betting web site, and I was largely (but not unconditionally) impressed with them all.

Android tablet and phone users are also catered for, but arguably not so well catered for just yet – which I put down to the fact that "city" types are more likely to sport iPhones than Android phones. I have previously reviewed Android apps provided by IG Index and Capital Spreads.

Android users need not despair if they cannot find a dedicated trading app for their chosen spread betting provider, because the Android web browser is able to run most if not all of the spread betting web interfaces due to the Android support for the Adobe Flash plug-in that is missing from the iOS (iPhone and iPad) operating system and which is crucial to fully utilising most of the spread betting companies' web sites.

If you can't find an Android app for your chosen spread betting provider, you might just about be able to operate their regular trading web site in an emergency – albeit rather clumsily if you're using a small screen smart phone rather than an Android tablet. If you're an iPhone or iPad user, you probably won't need to as you'll more than likely find a dedicated app.

Example Apps

It is not my intention here to give a blow-by-blow account of how the mobile trading apps work, because this will differ from provider to provider (although many of them are startlingly similar) and will also change over time. My intention in the following screenshots is merely to give you a feel for what the mobile trading apps look like.

My first example is the Capital Spreads Android app, and in particular the "Positions" screen that lists your "in play" spread bets. In the following screenshot notice how your overall account standing is also displayed on the screen.

Capital Spreads Android App "Positions" screen courtesy of Capital Spreads (prices are indicative)

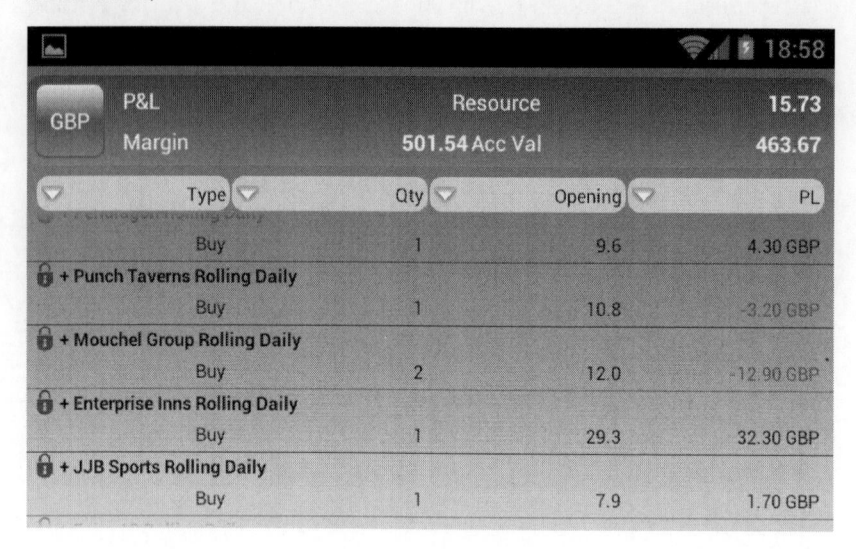

					18:58
GBP	P&L		Resource		15.73
	Margin		501.54 Acc Val		463.67
	Type	Qty		Opening	PL
	Buy	1		9.6	4.30 GBP
+ Punch Taverns Rolling Daily					
	Buy	1		10.8	-3.20 GBP
+ Mouchel Group Rolling Daily					
	Buy	2		12.0	-12.90 GBP
+ Enterprise Inns Rolling Daily					
	Buy	1		29.3	32.30 GBP
+ JJB Sports Rolling Daily					
	Buy	1		7.9	1.70 GBP

My next example is the IG Index "Market Detail" screen that for a particular market (i.e. a financial instrument such as an individual equity) combines a chart with the current buying and selling prices. Dealing in the particular market via the Deal Ticket or Order Ticket is just a screen-tap away.

IG Index Android App "Market Detail" screen courtesy of IG Index (prices are indicative)

Mobile App vs. Web Interface

The mobile trading apps make good use of the more limited smart phone screen real estate, and in general they provide most of the functionality provided by the traditional browser-based web interfaces.

There may be a limited number of functions – such as depositing and withdrawing funds – that can only be accomplished using the spread betting providers' web interfaces, and the mobile apps are typically "modal" in operation such that you can only do one thing at a time whereas the spread betting web interfaces often allow multiple windows and multiple trading tickets to be displayed simultaneously.

It may not be time to throw out the PC just yet, and the mobile trading apps might best be regarded as a complement rather than a replacement for the spread betting companies' full-blown trading interfaces, but they constitute a credible complement for those who wish to trade on the move.

Chapter Summary

At the outset I invited you to think of the "tools of the trade" as the various controls and indicators that help you drive your car. Mastery of those controls is necessary but is not sufficient when it comes to being a better driver, and it's the same with spread betting too. As well as understanding how to use the *tools of the trade* you also need to master some of the *tricks of the trade*. So that's what we'll look at in Chapter 5 – Tricks of the Trade.

5 – Tricks of the Trade

Building on the previous chapter that discussed the *tools of the trade*, in this chapter I'll share with you some *tricks of the trade* (pun intended) that might help you become a better spread bettor. If the tools of the trade are like the controls of your car, then learning the tricks of the trade may make you a better driver, notwithstanding the fact that you will still be at the mercy of the market's driving conditions.

Dread the Spread

I've been there and I've done it. I mean that I have rushed into pressing the "buy" button without noticing that my "investment" will become 40% less valuable as soon as I have committed to it, because I didn't notice that the bid-ask spread on Allied Irish Banks (for example) was a massive 0.05 - 0.08. In this case, it would mean that the share price must rise by 60% for you even to break even on your purchase.

In general it's better to trade markets that have narrow spreads so that you're not at an instant disadvantage, so it's no wonder that the spread betting companies often boast about their *tight spreads*. Often those boasts about tight spreads refer to the highly liquid markets that they would like you to be day-trading, such as stock indices, commodities and foreign exchange currency pairs. When it comes to individual equities, the spreads might not be so tight and you'll need to double-check on a case-by-case basis just before you press the "buy" (or "sell") button.

In some cases you may be willing to accept a wide spread in exchange for the massive upside potential that you see. Whereas a stock like Tesco may have a bid-ask spread of just 318-319 (less than 1%), you might consider it to be far less likely than Allied Irish Banks to become a "ten-bagger" (a stock whose price rises tenfold). If a stock rises tenfold over the longer position trading timescale then an initial 40% hit on the bid-ask spread may be neither here nor there. But it will matter a great deal (and lead to a not-so-great deal) if you're planning on closing the trade within a day.

The bottom line: double-check the bid-ask spread before you commit to the trade, but take account of your trading timescale.

Mind the Gap!

It's no fun to see one of your stock holdings fall in price unexpectedly and far, apparently instantaneously without giving you time to think let alone close your position. If you don't know what a price gap looks like, it looks something like this:

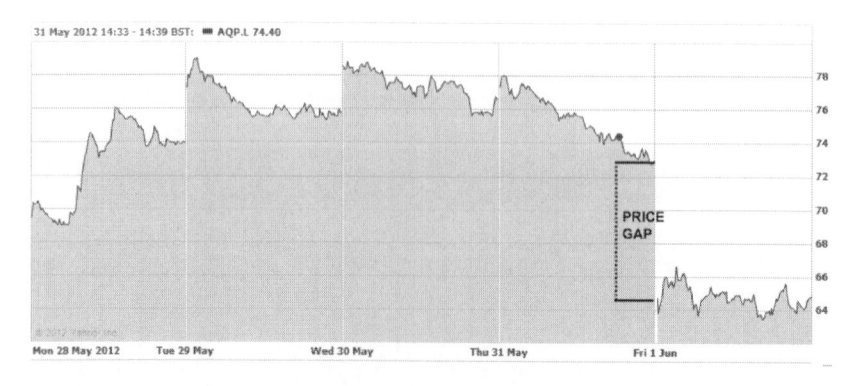

Aquarius Platinum Chart courtesy of Yahoo! Finance

Do you see how, overnight, the price dropped from about 73p-per-share to about 65p-per-share without apparently passing through the prices in between? Any non-guaranteed stop order that you had put in place at 71p would likely have been executed at the lower 65p-per-share, losing you six points unexpectedly and leaving you "out of position" (i.e. no longer holding the stock) for any possible rebound.

When these kinds of price gaps occur, even my weapon of choice (the stop order) cannot save you, and it may be detrimental because you may find that you need not have stopped out at all. But don't count on this, as the price may go even lower!

There is no cast iron solution to the price-gap problem, but there are some things you can try to at least part-mitigate the risk:

- A **guaranteed stop order** at the 71p price level would certainly have executed at that price, but due to the necessarily wider stop distance you could only have guaranteed your stop at that level when the price was up at around 78p-per-share. On spread betting platforms like IG Index you would have needed to guarantee the stop order at the time you opened the original trade, whereas on the Capital Spreads (and possibly InterTrader) platforms you could have guaranteed your existing stop order at a later time... but obviously not after the price gap had occurred!

- You might **anticipate the gap** (or the possibility of one occurring) by not leaving trades open overnight when most price gaps are likely to occur; which is exactly what day traders do.

- You might **temporarily remove or relax your stop order** before the markets open if you have read pre-open news that is likely to lead to a temporary adverse price gap. This is one of the very few situations in which it might be advisable to widen a stop order, and it's risky, but you might have little to lose if you expect the price to "gap through" your stop order anyway. Don't forget to return your stop order to a more appropriate level as soon as the price has settled down!

- One of the best protections against price gaps that I have found is **diversification**. By holding a diverse set of individual equity positions, and by not letting any of those positions grow disproportionately large, you can ensure that no one price gap can ever wipe you out.

We can't prevent price gaps from occurring, but these stop-gap solutions might help to mitigate their effects.

Averaging Down (Safely)

Many new spread bettors may be tempted to "double-up" their stake in a losing position on the basis that this will lower their average cost of ownership and will lower the price at which their combined position will "break even". If you stake £1-per-point at a price of 100 and another £1-per-point at a lower price of 50 then – hey presto – the price only needs to recover to 75 in order for you to break even and close the bets.

Note that one of the problems with this strategy is that novice spread bettors have a tendency to breathe a sigh of relief and take back the cash as soon as they have broken even in this scenario. So in the best outcome they make no profit, and in the worst outcome the bets become worthless.

While a surprising number of traditional investment books advocate the "average down" strategy, most successful traders will agree that it is usually better simply to let the losers go while running the winners. At worst those losers could fall all the way to zero and take an increasing amount of your cash with them, and at best the losers are tying up cash that might be better deployed elsewhere.

In a longer-term position trading strategy rather than a quick-fire day trading strategy there may be some justification for holding onto falling stocks using small stake sizes, and there may even be some justification for "averaging down" on a losing position providing you do so safely. Which begs the question: "How do you average down safely?"

One answer to this question is to average down uniformly across a large number of diverse positions so that no one position becomes a magnet for your cash. If the price of stock A falls by half, and you average down, think about averaging down stock B when this stock halves in price before you think about averaging down stock A yet again.

Another answer to the question is to take on less additional risk each time you average down.

Suppose you establish a £1-per-point position on a low-price stock at just 20p-per-share, for a risk of £20. This volatile "penny stock" halves in price to just 10p-per-share, so an additional "averaged down" position at £1-per-point will add a lesser £10-worth of risk. When the price halves again to just 5p-per-share you can add yet another £1-per-point position for an additional risk of only £5.

The beauty of this approach is that it protects against a single losing position becoming a magnet for all of your cash, because: the more the price falls, the less additional risk capital you commit. Yet it is more cost-effective than (in this case) having committed the full £3-per-point at the outset.

Note that this approach to averaging down safely can be implemented on higher-price stocks, indices and commodities too if we think of it in terms of the risk-to-stop. A £1-per-point spread bet on the FTSE 100 index at 6000 with a tight stop order at 5980 risks £20, and when the index price falls to 5990 an additional £1-per-point bet with the same stop order at 5980 risks just £10, and so on in ever-decreasing amounts.

This is different from how a traditional investor might average down by making an equal-value investment – let's say £1000 each time – whenever the stock halves in price, thereby doubling his capital-at-risk on the second go. It is also the opposite of what some novice speculators might be tempted to do, which is to invest increasingly higher amounts (god forbid) each time the price falls, in a desperate attempt to get back to "break even" even sooner. This is an example of a Martingale money management strategy that I'll describe in the next chapter.

Pyramiding

Pyramiding means adding additional funds to an existing position when it moves in the right direction; thereby causing you to benefit even more if the price continues to move in the right direction. Pyramiding is a way of "backing the winners" that seems completely contrary to the more common practice (among newcomers) of "averaging down" the losers.

Here is a graphical example of what difference it could make to the eventual return by pyramiding from £1-per-point to £2-per-point at the right time by placing a second £1-per-point bet:

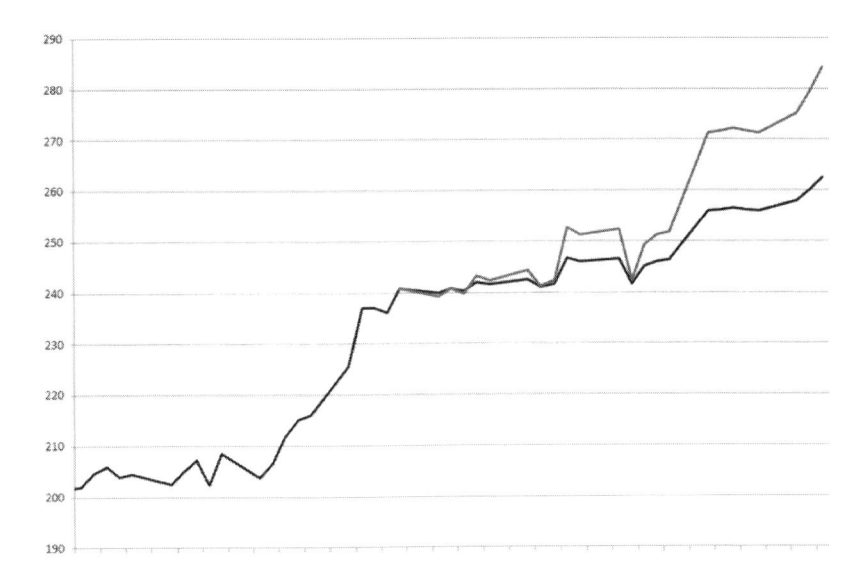

There is no sure-fire rule for when it is best to pyramid, but from a risk management perspective a good rule of thumb is to never pyramid until the profit on the original position is greater than the risk of the new position – so that, in the worst case, you will at least have broken even. This is best demonstrated via a concrete example.

Pyramiding Example

In the following example for Enterprise Inns (which was a real-life pyramided trade) you can see how a first £1-per-point spread bet was opened at a price of 29p-per-share on 28 December 2011 and then a second £1-per-point spread bet was opened at a price of 51p-per-share on 6 March 2012. The net result is that the 22-point price move notched up between those two dates amounted to £22, and the smaller additional 16-point price move from 6 March until the end of the chart amounted to a larger £32. In total, a 38-point move generated a £54 paper profit.

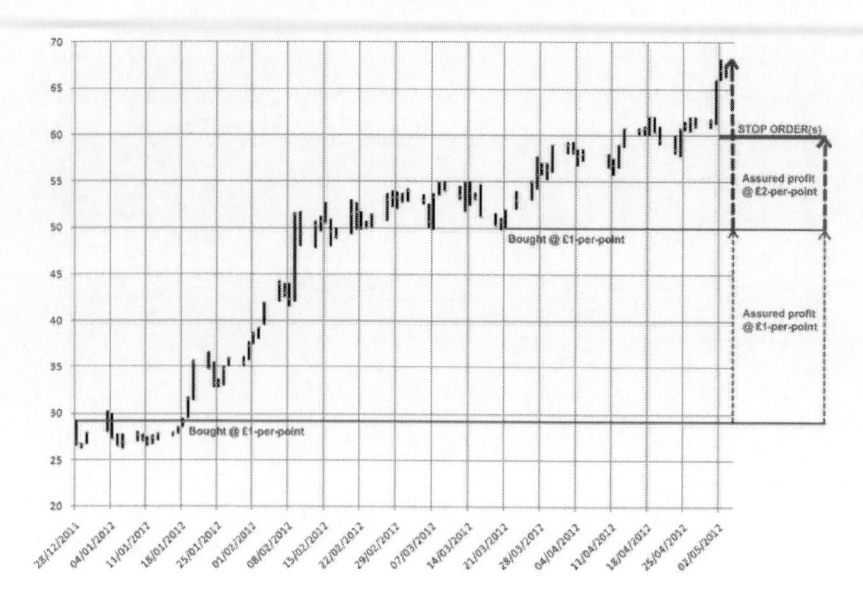

At this point the £54 profit is not assured if the price falls back, but £34 of it is assured thanks to the stop order that has been raised to 57p-per-share in order to "lock in" some profit on both positions. If the price falls back then the first £1-per-point position is expected to stop-out for a profit of £28 and the second position is expected to stop out for a profit of £6, but those profits are only really assured if a guaranteed stop order has been used.

Some of the more gung-ho traders would point out that an original spread bet at £2-per-point would have generated a larger £76 paper profit, of which £56 would be assured by the stop order. Ah yes, but at double the initial risk for not double the profit. Pyramiding is less risky than betting the farm in the first place because you should not pyramid a second position at all unless the new risk-to-stop is more than covered by the assured profit on the original position.

More about Pyramiding

The pyramiding strategy will be most relevant to longer term position traders, but not all spread bettors will be position traders. The potential (or actual) day traders and swing traders among you will be glad to know that I have relegated a more in-depth discussion of pyramiding to my position trading book.

How to make a Whipsaw Profit

Whipsaw losses are the losses that you notch up by repeatedly buying high and selling low, which as we all know is exactly the opposite of what you should be doing. They occur like this:

You buy the FTSE 100 index (for example) at the 5000 price level with a protective stop order at 4900. You get stopped out, losing you £100, and the price rises again to 5000. Thinking that you stopped out for no good reason, you re-establish your long position at 5000 out of 'fear of missing out' on what must surely now be an up-trend. The price falls back again, triggers your stop order and loses you another £100, rises back to 5000 and you buy in again. And so on and so forth, as the index trades sideways in a 100-point range.

Few spread bettors realise that it is also possible to notch up "whipsaw profits" when a trade goes the wrong way and then promptly reverses after stopping you out. I discovered this phenomenon by accident while running a spread betting account that mandated the use of guaranteed stop orders on all trades – whether you liked it or not. (The account in question was a "Shorts & Longs" account which has now been absorbed into the mother company SpreadEx).

Consider the scenario depicted in the following chart. Take a look at the chart, and then I'll explain what happened.

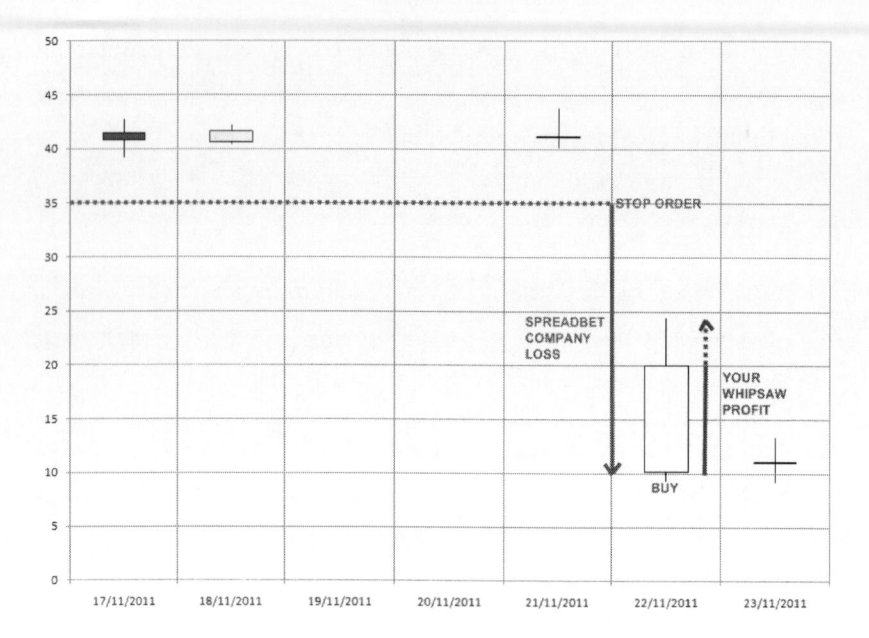

Overnight on 21 November 2011 the price of this stock "gapped down" from around 40p-per-share to just 10p-per-share. Because the trader had a guaranteed stop order at 35p, the spread betting company took a loss of 25 points when it closed the position. Having been stopped-out at 35p-per-share this canny trader immediately re-bought at the lower 10p-per-share and notched up a "whipsaw profit" when the price rebounded by between 10 and 15 points to part-close the gap. In a sense, then, it was the spread betting company and not the trader that got whipsawed out of the trade at a loss.

It gets better, because when a price gaps down like this the spread betting company will not necessarily stop you out at all at the lower price. They're not really breaking their promise here because if they do stop you out then it has to be at your guaranteed price level, but they don't have to stop you out until they have seen whether or not the price rebounds. This can work to your advantage if your original trade is left "in play" when you establish a second position at the gapped-down price and subsequently get to run a profit on both positions.

Your Trading Plan

If you fail to plan, you plan to fail.

Once you understand the tricks of the trade and have decided on the ones that will work for you, and perhaps discovered a few of your own, it is important to formulate them into a trading plan. Your trading plan will tell you (or remind you) exactly what to do in each situation, so that you are not wracked by emotion and indecision when the time comes to take the required action.

Your trading plan should answer questions like:

- What proportion of your trading funds will you allocate to each serial trade or parallel position?

- What will you do when a trade goes against you? Close it down for a small loss, or increase your stake?

- What will you do when a trade goes in your favour? Take you profit quickly, or run the profit while pyramiding additional funds?

- How will you guard against the potentially devastating effects of price gaps? By diversifying, by applying guaranteed stop orders, or both?

The Life Cycle of a Trade

When devising a trading plan it is useful to think in terms of the full lifecycle of a trade. Some of the trading literature, and much of the investment literature, implies that profitable speculation it is all about clever stock (or other asset) picking; i.e. your *trade entries*.

For all traders and especially for day traders and swing traders – *trade exits* are just as important as the *trade entries*. For longer-term position traders, *trade maintenance* by pyramiding additional funds or trailing your stop orders becomes just as important and entry and exit. So make sure your trading plan takes account of each of the boxes – Entry, Maintenance and Exit – shown in the graphic below.

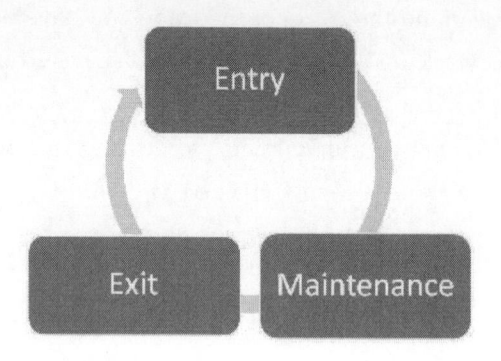

Sample Trading Plan

Here is a sample trading plan that encompasses the aspects mentioned above plus other aspects that should be covered by a trading plan. It may be based roughly on *my trading plan*, but it doesn't have to (and probably shouldn't) become *your trading plan*.

What to Trade: Only individual equities; no indices, commodities or currencies.

When to Trade (Trade Entry): On market weakness, in stocks which have suffered a short-term price shock but which have good long-term potential.

Position Sizing: Start each position with the minimum allowable spread bet size, with a view to pyramiding a larger position over time.

Stop Orders: Always (and only) apply a stop order when the risk-to-0 is potentially catastrophic, but always apply a stop order as soon as it is possible to lock-in some profit.

Pyramiding: Make additional bets only when (but not merely because) the existing locked-in profit exceeds the new risk.

Diversification: While concentrating on UK equities, hold as many separate positions as possible so that no single company-specific adverse event can be fatal.

Averaging Down: Always average down across-the-board, and do so with less risk each time by placing same-size spread bets at lower prices.

Trade Exit: Never sell out manually except to partial-close a position at the top of a swing while leaving the remainder to run for higher profit. Otherwise allow profit-securing stop orders to close positions.

As I have already hinted: don't treat this as a concrete trading plan for you to follow. It might not work for you and your trading mentality, and it might not continue to work for me either. But I have a plan that leaves me in no doubt about what to do in any given situation, and so should you.

Chapter Summary

In this chapter we have considered some of the trading techniques or "tricks of the trade" that complement the "tools of the trade" that were discussed in the previous chapter. Whereas the tools of the trade will enable you to drive the trade, the tricks of the trade will help you to become a better driver.

The chapter concluded with a sample trading plan that combines elements of the "tricks of the trade" and which takes the emotion out of trading by telling you exactly what to do under various trading circumstances. Not that the sample trading plan was intended to tell *you* what to do *exactly*.

6 – Risk Doesn't Have To Be Risky

If I asked you what is the most important aspect of your spread betting system, it's likely that many of you would say "finding the right trade set-ups", which is what we'll look at shortly in the next chapter. But you'd be wrong.

Identifying the very best trading opportunities won't save you from ultimately visiting the poor house if you fail to manage your downside (and for that matter, upside) risk properly. I really believe that if you look after the downside, the upside will pretty much take care of itself. To put it bluntly: you can't ensure or even predict that your latest penny stock pick will become a ten-bagger, but you can ensure that it doesn't take your whole account down with it if it goes bust.

Professional poker players know "when to hold, and when to fold", and that's how they make money consistently over time. Great golfers are not the ones who hit the biggest shots, but the ones who make the fewest mistakes.

Risk management is so important that it deserves a chapter all of its own, and this chapter deserves to come before the one in which we attempt to identify good trading opportunities. But before we talk about risk management, we need to clear up the possible confusion between risk management and money management. They're similar, but not the same.

Money Management and Risk Management

Money management is often the last thing on the mind of the new spread bettor who is looking to make big money with very little effort. If you bet big you might win big, but sooner or later you will go bust. Let me explain using the analogy of a casino.

The casino's roulette wheel is biased very slightly in favour of the house, giving them a slight edge of (let's say) 51% of the time they win and 49% of the time one of their clients wins. This very slight edge means that the casino is statistically guaranteed to come out ahead and make money in the long run over a large number of bets. But the casino owner is still in danger of going bust if he allows a single "high roller" client to place a single big bet equivalent to the casino's cash pile. So they don't allow it, and they take a more actuarial approach to making small amounts of sure money over time.

In a similar fashion, a good spread bettor can make sure money over time with only a slight "edge" in the market stemming from good strategy; as long as he (or she) is never tempted to "bet the farm" on just one spin of the metaphorical roulette wheel. In short, a spread bettor should think more like the casino owner than the casino punter – by practising sound money management.

What this means in practice is risking a mere fraction of your available funds on any one bet, commonly (for successful spread bettors) as low as just 1% of available funds. It means "risking" just £10 on each serial or parallel bet in a £1000 spread betting account. On this basis no one bad bet can ever wipe you out, and you can also survive the inevitable extended run of bad luck that you will surely suffer at some point. The simple calculation is that you can suffer up to 100 losses in a row at £10 per loss before your £1000 trading funds run out, but sound money management is yet more subtle...

Martingale and Anti-Martingale Money Management

Here's a strategy that was popular among casino players in 18th century France and which is popular among novice spread bettors today:

When you bet £100 on the roulette wheel, and you lose, the next time you should bet £200, and the next time £400, and so on. Assuming 50/50 odds, you would only need your last (biggest) bet to come good in order to recover all of your prior losses... and more. This is the Martingale strategy that sounds seductive but which is fatally flawed.

If you hit a losing streak of nine bad bets in a row, which is perfectly possible, then on your tenth turn you would find yourself betting more than £50,000. Which is a far cry from your £100 initial bet, and I bet (pun intended) that this – plus the "almost as much" that you have already bet in total – is more money than you took into the casino. So it's "Game Over" in just ten turns.

Although the Martingale strategy may indeed come good eventually when betting on stock indices, which unlike individual equities can't conceivably go all the way to zero, most seasoned spread bettors know that their pockets are not deep enough to sustain the exponentially increasing bet sizes. So, in fact, they practice a form of anti-Martingale betting in which they bet less and less as their trading funds diminish.

Fixing an amount-per-bet at 10% (but it's more likely to be just 1%) of available trading funds has an in-built automatic stabilizer. When you lose £100 of your £1,000 cash balance, the 10% rule ensures that next time you will stake only £90. After losing twice in a row you will stake only £81, and so on.

If you follow an anti-Martingale strategy, you won't make a killing when your final big bet comes good; but at least you'll 'stay in the game' long enough to realise your trading edge... if you have one.

So much for *money management*, but this chapter is meant to be about *risk management*. So let's continue with the question...

What is Risk Anyway?

In simple terms, risk is the amount of money that you stand to lose (the impact) if a trade goes wrong. A £1-per-point bet on a stock index priced at 5000 notionally places £5000 at risk, regardless of the spread betting company asking you to put up a much lower amount or margin to take the trade. But you know that stock indices do not generally "go bust" and so you assess the probability of a total wipe-out to be a mere 1%. Arguably, a notional value-at-risk can be calculated as £5000 x 1% = £50.

Obviously there are a range of possible outcomes, like the probability of losing half of your money if the index halves in value, but stick with me and my total wipe-out scenario for the sake of argument.

By placing a guaranteed stop order at 100 points below your buying price, you can reduce your worst-case monetary risk from £5000 down to just £100. But with (let's say) a 50% probability of getting stopped-out on a more likely 100-point price fall, your notional risk would come out the same at £100 * 50% = £50.

Don't take these calculations too literally. I'm just introducing you to the idea that true financial risk (and any risk) may be calculated as:

risk = probability * impact

Events that have a high likelihood of occurring, and which will have a devastating impact if they do, are very risky; like betting the whole farm on a company that might be in the process of going bust. In this case you need to reduce the risk by either a) reducing the **probability** of an adverse outcome by choosing a more stable stock, or b) reducing the **impact** of an adverse outcome by staking a small fraction of your available cash.

Risk Cuts Both Ways

This might surprise you, but true financial risk also includes the possibility that something "good" might happen. The penny share that has a 50% probability of going bust might also have a 50% probability of doubling in value... or more. And the more you stake, the bigger will be the positive impact on your cash balance if it does, according to the same calculation:

positive risk = probability (of a good event) * **impact** (dependent on the amount you staked)

Before you go betting the farm on that penny share tip after all, let me bring you back down to earth. If ever you bet the farm, and you lose, then it's Game Over. Regardless of the potential glory, your main priority at all times must be to "stay in the game". Look after the downside risk and let the upside-risk take care of itself.

Volatility and Risk

In this chapter I will be focussing on "risk", which is not the same thing as "volatility". The price of a financial instrument may be volatile, but betting on it need not be risky. Volatility may in fact increase the "positive" risk, which is exactly what you need in order to make money.

What to do About Risk

In the simplest terms there are two things you can do about risk:

- Lessen your exposure to risk through *mitigation*.
- Have a *contingency* plan for when a risk materializes.

Mitigation

Given what I said earlier about risk being a product of both *probability* and *impact*, you can mitigate risks by:

- Reducing the probability of an adverse event such as a *price gap*, by only betting on highly liquid indices and major currencies rather than penny stocks.
- Lessening the impact of an adverse outcome by using *prudent position sizing* or by applying stop orders.

The irony with stop orders is that the tighter the stop, the higher the probability of taking a loss but the lower the impact will be. So there is an inherent trade-off between probability and impact when deciding on stop distances.

Contingency

It's all very well trying to reduce the probability of an adverse event, and lessening the potential impact, but what will you do if the worst does happen? What is your contingency plan?

If one of your big bets goes sour and takes your entire account balance with it, will you dust yourself down and try again or will you skulk off back to the day job with your tail between your legs? Actually, this may not be such a bad idea, but on the assumption that you'll try again let's consider another scenario.

When one of your positions stops out at a loss, when would you consider re-entering the same position? When the price starts rising again (thus risking a second "whipsaw" loss) or only if the price falls even further (which is my favourite, but that day may never come)?

Other Ways to Manage Risks

If you read a book dedicated to risk management, which will surely send you to sleep, you will discover that there are at least three more ways of managing risks:

- You might *avoid* the risk by not spread betting at all.

- You might *accept* the risk by buying and blindly holding your positions... possibly all the way to zero.

- You might *transfer* the risk, for example by applying a "guaranteed" stop order to your bet.

Oh, heck, I just thought of another one. My personal favourite risk management strategy is to...

Diversify the Danger Away

Guaranteed stop orders can be useful when they are available, when the costs are acceptable for the protection being afforded, and when the minimum stop distances do not cause the protection to be placed beyond the point of usefulness. Where guaranteed stop orders are not available, not affordable, or not appropriate we need to think of something else.

Money management and prudent position sizing come in here, but they are often thought about in serial terms: a day trader risks no more than 1% of available funds on the "current" trade before moving onto the next one. Any given trade cannot wipe him out.

Traditional investors don't think in terms of serial trades, but in terms of parallel positions, and so do I. While always retaining some spare firepower for when it is most needed, I'm not afraid of deploying a significant proportion of my available trading funds all at once – so long as I do so in diverse set of positions. This actuarial approach to spreading risk will be familiar to traditional investors, yet it is entirely compatible with spread betting.

When Many Baskets are Only One

You might think that you can save yourself a lot of hassle by deploying all of your trading funds into a "diversified" FTSE 100 spread bet on the assumption that you are spreading your eggs across many baskets exactly as in my example above. But you're not.

When you place a single bet on the FTSE 100 index you are actually putting all of your eggs into just one basket: the FTSE 100 basket. You have to buy the index all in one go, and sell it all in one go, with no ability whatsoever to time the purchases and sales of the individual constituents.

Can You Afford The Risk?

When you woke up on 14 May 2012 you may have been happy to read the news that "Sony shares tumble to 31-year low amid record losses". Happy because this would be your chance to take punt on a world-class company that was now trading price-wise at one tenth of its former glory. This could turn out to be the bet-of-the-decade, but could you afford to take it?

Whereas in a multi-thousand pound account this should not be a problem, in your "starter account" capitalised at £1000 and with your 1% money management criteria mandating a risk of no more than £10 per trade this trade may simply be unaffordable. This is because, although the price of Sony shares shown on Yahoo! Finance and Google Finance charts would have been in the order of 15, the price displayed by your spread betting company would most likely be 100x higher (not that it's really a different price) at 1500. On a minimum £1-per-point bet your £10 maximum risk would imply a stop order at 1490, and this doesn't even account for the additional five-point bid-ask spread. A stop order placed this close to the current price is highly probable to stop out, especially since the price had fallen by almost 7% the previous day.

In order to stay within your money management criteria in this case you would need to employ a very tight stop (with a high probability of stopping-out) or a much wider distance-to-stop (with a high impact of say 100 points if it does stop out). But you can't afford a £100 risk on a single trade in a £1000 account, not least because the true worst-case risk (if the company goes bust overnight) is actually £1500!

In this scenario you would have to take a rain check on the potentially lucrative trade and look for something with a lower price a little closer to home. Unless you were willing to recapitalise your account, relax your money management criteria... or simply take a risk (not recommended), that is.

Learning to Love Leverage

Some people get awfully excited about leverage, and not in a good way, but sometimes I can't help wondering "What's all the fuss about leverage?"

If you are a homeowner or buy-to-let property owner then you are also almost certainly leveraged. For example, if you bought a £1,000,000 house using a £200,000 deposit then you're leveraged by a factor of 5. If house prices fell by just 20% then 'on paper' your asset would have lost £200,000 of its value and your deposit investment has notionally been wiped out entirely. Even worse, if the house burnt down and you'd forgotten to insure it, then you would lose five times your original investment and would receive a 'margin call' (in all but name) from the mortgage lender for the balance of £800,000!

Most people have been in this sort of position, and so they manage their leverage by a) insuring the bigger house or b) buying a less expensive £200,000 house using a £40,000 deposit and a £160,000 mortgage while keeping the same £160,000 on deposit – ideally at a high rate of interest – just in case it is ever needed to settle the mortgage.

It's exactly the same with spread betting whereby you can make the equivalent of a £1,000 "investment" using a £200 deposit (for example) and using the remaining £800 risk capital provided by the spread betting company in exchange for their financing charges. If the full £1000 that you are truly "risking" is too rich for your blood then just *don't do it*, or apply a guaranteed stop order to reduce your risk to a more manageable level, or deploy a much lower £40 deposit so as to risk only the "leveraged up" £200 that you can truly afford to risk.

A Leveraged Misunderstanding

I read recently on a popular investment web site the tale of an investor whose first foray into spread betting lost him his entire £250 deposit on a £2,500-equivalent investment in Aviva shares. By my reckoning he lost exactly the same amount that he would have lost on a £2,500 Aviva investment in a traditional share dealing account – no more, no less – simply because the share price fell. And yet he vowed to walk away from spread betting.

Interestingly, one guy who commented on the article (or perhaps who commented on my comment about the article) at suggested that *"it is a mistake to assume that all spread-betters are day traders buying on margin"* and I agree. He went on to explain how an investor with

£100K to invest in shares could purchase these by depositing £10K in a spread-betting account (at 10% margin) and could put the remaining £90K in a high-interest account. This makes spread betting a very low cost way of trading because interest from the 90k residual deposit should offset interest charges from the SB account.

The original article that I am referring to was published at http://www.fool.co.uk/news/investing/2012/06/01/trading-your-way-to-a-million-or-not.aspx

The Bottom Line on Leverage

The bottom line is that spread betting and other leveraged trading is not inherently more risky than other forms of investment because, hey, the leverage is only a multiplying factor. The secret to loving leverage is this:

If your chosen financial instrument is leveraged at 5x, then just stake one-fifth of your intended amount. Or take out insurance in the form of a guaranteed stop order.

It really is that simple. But you might still be wondering...

Margin Calls: Can I Lose More than My Initial Deposit?

Yes you can. If you deposited £100 with the spread betting company and found this amount to be sufficient (thanks to leverage) for placing a £10-per-point bet on a single 100p-per-share stock (total risk=£1000), and if this company went bust overnight, you would find yourself owing the spread betting company the balance of £900 that you hadn't deposited; unless you had fixed your risk absolutely at £100 by placing a guaranteed stop order at 90p-per-share.

In a less extreme example: if the price of that particular stock halved overnight you would find yourself owing the spread betting company an additional £400 that you had not deposited originally. In the past, it may have been likely for you to receive a "margin call" – a telephone call or email urging you to deposit additional funds immediately in order to keep your losing position open. In reality, these days it is much more likely that the spread betting company will liquidate the position (and any others that you hold) in order to settle as much of the debt as possible; and then call you for the rest of the money.

Even in the normal course of events you may find yourself at various times receiving some form of "Liquidation Warning" email containing words along these lines:

"Please take this email as notification that the funds on your account are now considerably below the margin requirements for your position(s).

...

Please make sure you take the appropriate action necessary to cover your margin, we may without further notice to you close all or part of your positions in order to take your account off call. Positions will be closed at the current market levels at the time we close them. You will be liable for any debit balances that may arise from the closure of the position(s) and this will be due immediately."

If you're quick enough, it may be possible to make good the shortfall before your open positions are closed, but it's better to be prepared by having an adequate surplus balance than to deposit additional funds in haste. Many good traders would advise you never to meet a margin call by depositing more cash, because maybe it's telling you something about how over-leveraged and under-diversified you are.

Counter-Party Risk

One of the commonly ignored risks is counter-party risk, or the risk that the spread betting company you are dealing with goes bust. This can happen, as former clients of MF Global and World Spreads are all too aware.

Diversification can play a role in reducing the counter-party risk. As well as diversifying across different equities and other financial markets, it may be a good idea to diversify across spread betting companies. Not only to guard against them going bust, but also to guard against a particular trading platform being unavailable when you must make that trade. You can find a list of spread betting companies in the appendix, but do keep in mind that ideally you would wish to diversify across *spread betting platforms* rather than merely *spread betting brands*. In this context Capital Spreads, InterTrader and possibly even ETX Capital run on essentially the same *London Capital Group* trading platform whereas IG Index runs on an entirely different trading platform.

The good news is that if you are classed as a retail client (which you most likely will be) in the UK, and if you hold an account valued at no more than £50,000 (correct at the time of writing) then you should be covered by the Financial Services Compensation Scheme (FSCS) in the event that your spread betting counter-party company goes to the wall; but it may take a little while for you to see the return of your cash as clients of MF Global and World Spreads discovered.

World Spreads Woes, and the FSCS Payout Timeline

16 March 2012: At close of business, spread betting company World Spreads was placed into special administration by the Financial Services Authority (FSA) due to accounting irregularities and amid suggestions of a shortfall in clients' funds.

30 March 2012: Administrators KPMG sent closing statements to clients of World Spreads and its white label spread betting partners (including Ladbrokes) in order to clarify the prospective claims from clients... who will have had all of their open positions closed and converted to a cash value.

19 June 2012: The administrators updated me to say that any payout from the Financial Services Compensation Scheme (FSCS) is likely to occur before the proposed "interim distribution to creditors" that is estimated to take place in September.

At the time of writing, I am confident that the FSCS will make good my loss from the World Spreads collapse, but this experience underlines the importance of spreading your risk by running accounts with several of the spread betting companies.

Don't Speculate with Money You Can Afford to Lose!

My advice *"Don't speculate with money you can afford to lose!"* flies in the face of the conventional advice that you should "only speculate with money you can afford to lose", so let me explain what I mean.

There was once a guy – okay, it was me – who had a very successful career in which he was making good money, had a flash car and so on. With that money burning a hole in his pocket, he decided to play the markets. You might be able to guess what's coming, and it's this:

"Because I could afford to lose a lot of money... I did!"

At that time it didn't really matter if I lost money on failed trades, because there was always more money I could use to feed my trading obsession. Until one day there wasn't, because I decided to quit the rat race to trade and write and run my own publishing enterprise full-time. So I had to learn about money and risk-management – fast!

The fact is: having a lot of money can make you complacent in the face of losses, in the same way that (as I understand it) having insurance can in some senses actually make you a worse driver rather than a better one. Without a safety net, we tend to be much more careful; with a beneficent paymaster we tend to succumb to moral hazard.

When starting out in spread betting it may well be best to assume an attitude of not being able to afford to lose any money at all, regardless of your wealth. This is consistent with Warren Buffett's two rules of investing:

- Rule #1 Don't Lose Money!

- Rule #2 Don't forget Rule #1

In the real world you *will lose money*, at least in the form of the immediate bid-ask spread. On longer term position trades you may well see your positions fall some way before they recover their lost ground. So while I don't take the "don't lose money" mantra absolutely literally, it has shaped the way that I approach spread betting, for example:

- I start all positions with small bet sizes, and only pyramid additional funds from accrued profits.

- When banking a profit of (let's say) £10,000 I would be most likely to place £9,000 of it in a safe place while re-staking just £1,000 in a new set of spread bets.

Of course, there is some relationship to your true wealth in the sense that a small bet for a multimillionaire may well be equivalent to an average punter's "life savings" of say £50,000. And maybe the former really can afford to lose it.

Losing Money and Drawing Down

Although I have suggested that you should at all times aim to keep your losses to an absolute minimum, when running certain trading styles – in particular, my preferred position trading style – you may find yourself drawn down (i.e. showing a loss) by a considerable amount for a significant amount of time until things "hopefully" turn around.

Arguably, you should not suffer such prolonged draw-downs when day trading because your aim is to make some profit each and every day. If your day trading losses are mounting then your trading strategy simply isn't working, although it is also possible to encounter a "run of bad luck" that produces a longer string of losing bets than you might think.

Back on the subject of position trading draw-downs, I have reproduced an equity curve below that shows how one of my spread betting accounts drew down by up to 50% from a starting valuation (initially all in cash) of £1,000 to an account valuation (in cash and open bets) that could be liquidated for only £500.

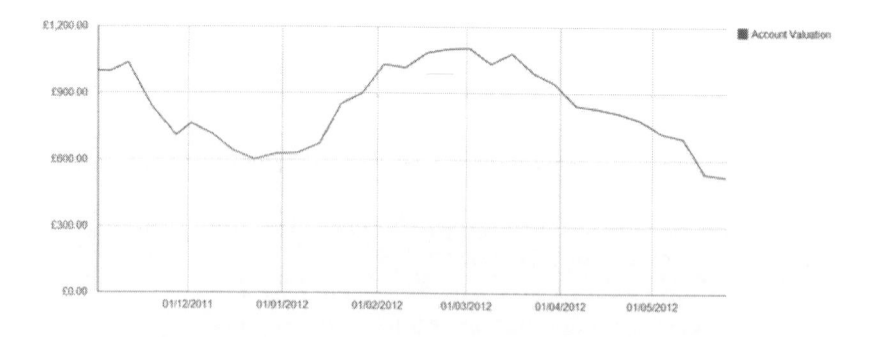

To a traditional investor this would look bad, very bad, because it implies the reduction in value of a hypothetical pension pot of £100,000 down to only £50,000. It may be a good reason to heed my earlier advice about using spread betting as a money making machine (even when position trading) that turns small amounts of money into large amounts of money rather than as a wealth preservation device for your accumulated life savings.

From a spread bettor's perspective, this draw down might not be as bad as it seems. To start with, it's a "paper loss" (because it will surely come back*) of only £500, and how many of us can't afford to lose just £500 over six months in the apparently dangerous world of spread betting?

*I'm joking a little here, because a paper loss should arguably be treated as seriously as a real loss.

The other reason that the draw down may not be as bad as it seems is because of the leverage. At the time of writing, one of my holdings chosen at random – let's choose Tesco – required a deposit of only £17 when priced at 314p-per-share. Thus my £17 deposit had afforded me the equivalent of a £314 "investment" in Tesco shares... because I stood to lose £314 (in the absence of a guaranteed stop order) if the company went bust. It means I was leveraged by some 18x, which if repeated across my entire portfolio meant that notionally my initial £1,000 deposit had afforded me £18,000 worth of "investing" power. When measured on this leveraged scale, a £500 interim loss on a total (equivalent) of £18,000 invested doesn't sound so bad; and it doesn't look so bad, either, in the following adjusted chart.

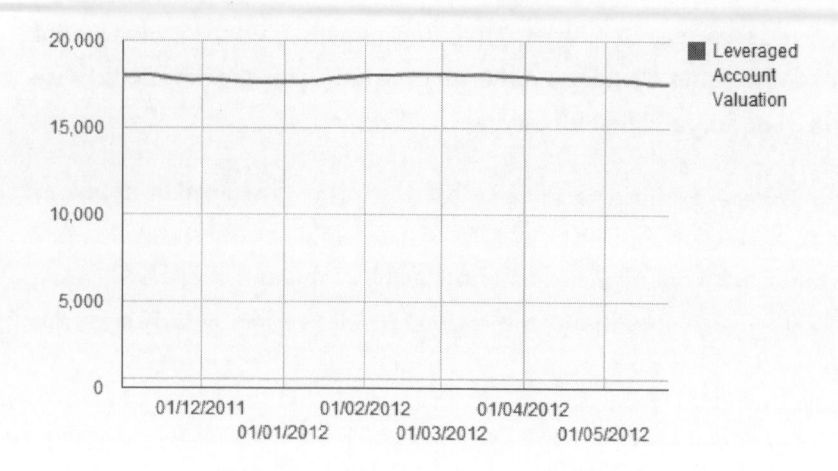

You may think that I have fiddled the figures here in order to paint a rosy picture, and I have to admit that any subsequent gains would look equally unimpressive on the second chart compared with on the first one. I should also stress that playing chart tricks like this, however plausible and reassuring it may seem, should not be treated as a justification for complacency in the face of mounting losses.

Trading Mistakes

One of the risks you run when spread betting is the risk that you will make mistakes. Trading mistakes can take many forms, and some of the most common ones are:

- You click the 'sell' button when you meant to click the 'buy' button, thereby going short instead of long.

- You place a bet on a commodity or foreign share in your spread betting account without first checking whether your £1-per-point bet will in fact be equivalent to £100-per-point because that particular instrument is priced per-0.01 units; hence you unintentionally increase your risk by a factor of 100.

- You sell a £4-per-point bet to close a long £5-per-point position, thereby leaving a residual (and unintentional) £1-per-point bet in play.

- You place a stop order at 100 points below the current price when you thought you were placing it at the 100p price level, because you mistook the 'stop distance' box for the "stop level" box on the trading ticket.

- You bet on a UK 100 December contract when you meant to bet on the UK 100 Rolling Daily, and you based your stop placement on the price chart for the latter.

These are some of the more common mistakes you can make, but by no means all of them. You'll discover several more of your own, which will lead you to the question of...

What to Do When You Make a Mistake

Experience has taught me that the best thing to do when you make a mistake is to immediately correct it by closing your unintentional position at a loss if necessary, rather than hanging on in there and hoping for the best.

Be sure to distinguish mistakes – i.e. things you did by accident that you never intended to do – from trades that simply went the wrong way. A failed trade is not a mistake of the kind I am talking about here.

Don't Worry, Be Happy!

A chapter devoted entirely to risk management is bound to have set alarm bells ringing in some spread bettors' minds. On the contrary, the message should be that if you master risk then you no longer need to worry about it.

An analogy: once you've passed your driving test and you take to the roads, you need to be aware that accidents can happen, but you need not be overly worried every time you get behind the wheel. Your tutor did teach you how to do an emergency stop, didn't he (or she)?

In order to encourage a healthy awareness of risk but not an obsessive worry about it, I draw on two inspirational quotes that I have culled from Dale Carnegie's (he of How to Win Friends and Influence People fame) other book How to Stop Worrying and Start Living.

The first quote is:

"For every ailment under the sun,
There is a remedy, or there is none;
If there be one, try to find it;
If there be none, never mind it."

The second quote is:

"God grant me the serenity
To accept the things I cannot change,
The courage to change the things I can;
And the wisdom to know the difference."

Finally, remember that – because risk cuts both ways – you need to accept some downside risk in order to enjoy the possibility of upside risk.

Chapter Summary

In this chapter I have focused on risk: what it is, and what to do about it. Risk management is of the utmost importance, and as I stated earlier: the even best very opportunity identification (e.g. clever stock picking) won't save you from an extended run of bad luck if you fail to manage your risk.

Not wishing to overly alarm you with my foregoing coverage, the important thing to remember is that *risk doesn't have to be risky!*

7 – Identifying Trading Opportunities

You may find it a little strange that I have left it so long to talk about identifying trading opportunities. Don't most trading and investment books make a big thing about telling you which stocks or other financial instruments to buy, and when? Well, I've left it until now for a very good reason. When trading or investing in general and particularly when spread betting, it is vitally important that you understand the *tools of the trade*, the *tricks of the trade*, and in particular the importance of *risk management* before you start splashing the cash.

While obviously I am aware of the many technical and fundamental techniques for identifying trading opportunities, my aim here is not to replicate the entire existing technical analysis and value investing literature. Rather, my intention is to share some of the opportunity identification strategies that I have found personally to be useful.

Bottom Fishing

Bottom fishing is one of my favourite sports, but it's not for everyone because you may be just as likely to hook yourself an old tyre or rusty bicycle as you are to land the prize fish lurking at the bottom of the pond.

Bottom fishing means looking for a bombed-out share that is priced at an all-time low and which you believe will subsequently recover. Because this is such a dangerous sport, I suggest the following:

- Try to identify stocks that have fallen massively today as well as over the long term. An immediate rebound will help you in your resolve to hold the stock for the long term potential, and will allow you to secure (with a stop order) or bank (by part-selling) some profit in the short term.

- Use an initial position size that you are willing (if not exactly "happy") to lose entirely; such as £1-per-point on a 50p-per-share stock, rather than £10-per-point on a 1000p-per-share stock. You can always "average down" (carefully) or "pyramid up" your position when you see which way it goes.

How to Discover Bottom Fishing Opportunities

Once way of identifying bottom fishing opportunities is to open the "Yahoo! Finance Price Losers (%)" list in your web browser via this web address:

http://uk.finance.yahoo.com/losers?e=ftas.

It will show you which stocks have fallen furthest today, and you can then click the chart link to see how the price fall fits into the context of a longer time perspective.

Another way to find bottom fishing opportunities is to watch the news. Big price falls are usually newsworthy and will make the headlines on the BBC News web site, on investment web sites such as The Motley Fool, and (of course) on your chosen spread betting company's own news feeds.

Bottom Fishing Example - "French Correction"

On the morning of 17 May 2012, French Connection (or should it be "French Correction"?) shares suffered a "correction" of some 25% when they fell from about 40p-per-share to about 30p-per-share. The following chart from Yahoo! Finance shows the longer-term price action, and "X" marks the spot at which the shares were priced on this particular morning.

Chart courtesy of Yahoo! Finance

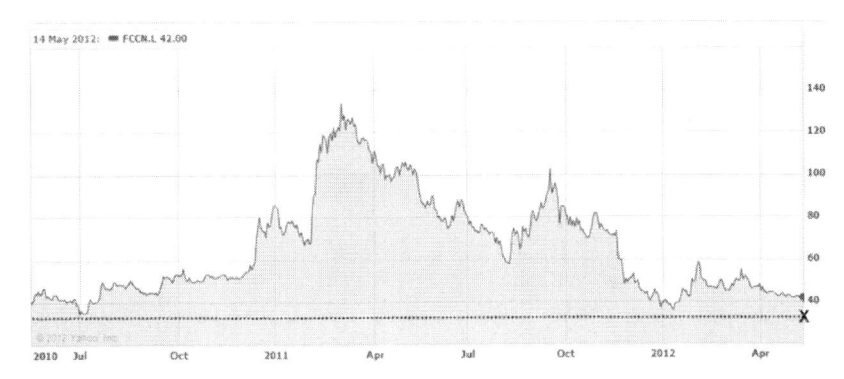

From a bottom fishing spread bettor's point of view, this stock may have been attractive at this point for a number of reasons:

- The sudden gap-down of 25% could lead to an immediate bounce-back profit for the day trader when the market realises that the correction has been overdone.

- Judging from what traders and investors thought the shares to be worth only a year earlier, the price potential may be attractive to a longer-term position trader.

- From a technical perspective, the price appears to have fallen to a support price – indicated by the dotted line – that has held on two previous occasions, making a rebound or recovery more likely... but by no means certain.

- From a "news" perspective, the latest price drop resulted from a third profit warning. Apparently, profit warnings always come in threes.

- From a personal perspective, a previous long bet that I had placed on French Connection had "stopped out" some weeks earlier at about 45p-per-share. So I would now be able to buy back, at a 33% discount, something that I had previously sold at a higher price thereby notionally "selling high and buying low" without having gone short.

There may also have been perfectly valid reasons for not taking the trade, such as the fact that any stock which falls 25% in a day can easily fall another 25% within a day; and any stock that has lost 80% of its value within a year can easily lose another 80%.

All things considered, the spread bettor would be wise in this case (as ever) to deploy a modest position size initially until he sees which way the price will go. Alternatively, he might apply a relatively tight stop order (ideally guaranteed) to a larger day trade position size.

How to Catch a Falling Knife

Many people advise against – or shy away from – bottom fishing, for fear of *trying to catch a falling knife*. Many spread bettors and other traders lose digits (not fingers, but trailing zeros from their bank balances) when they attempt this feat of daring, but I think it's because they're doing it all wrong because they:

- Try to grab too soon, when the knife has only just started falling.

- Grab too hard by making a big initial investment.

- Grab too doggedly, with no intention of letting go.

My suggestions for trying to catch a falling knife are:

- Try to catch a knife that has fallen rather than one which is still falling. Has the price of this financial instrument fallen a long way, and does it look like it's bounced off the floor?

- Grab cautiously at first using the light grip of a small position size. Your fingers may still get cut, but the lacerations won't be too deep.

- If the price keeps falling, let go, possibly automatically using a stop order that you placed just below what you thought was the floor level. Subsequently you can try to grab again with your other hand.

- Once you've got a firm grip, tighten it by increasing your position size as you lift the fallen knife from the ground.

Top Fishing

It's only logical that whereas long traders might engage in a spot of bottom fishing, short traders might try their hands at "top fishing". If you thought that Apple shares or the price of Gold (for example) had inflated to bubble-like proportions, or that Facebook shares had been massively overpriced at the time of flotation, you could just as easily go short in a spread betting account by selling as you could go long by buying.

Top Fishing Example

My top fishing concrete example takes the form of a fixed-odds binary bet of the kind offered by BetOnMarkets rather than a traditional spread bet. On 27 April 2012 I received an £80 payout (see below) from a short silver bet that I had placed one year earlier when I judged the price of silver to have "topped out". Granted, it's not big money, but it represented a 70% return on the £47 that I had staked when I placed the bet.

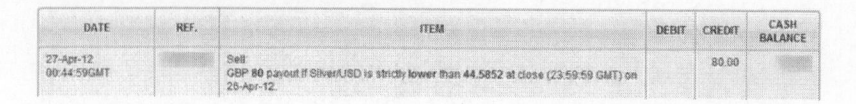

DATE	REF.	ITEM	DEBIT	CREDIT	CASH BALANCE
27-Apr-12 00:44:59GMT		Sell GBP 80 payout if Silver/USD is strictly lower than 44.5852 at close (23:59:59 GMT) on 28-Apr-12.		80.00	

The reasons I used a fixed-odds binary bet rather than a spread bet to back my judgement in this case are that a) it was more affordable, and b) my total risk was fixed absolutely. These reasons lead us nicely on to...

Top Fishing Terrors

While in one sense top fishing is the exact mirror image of bottom fishing, it is in several senses more dangerous and terrifying because:

Any financial instrument that has apparently "topped out" will be priced much higher than one that has apparently bottomed out. A topped-out stock at 1000p-per-share is obviously much more likely to move 100 points against you than a bottomed out stock at 10p-per-share.

While the price of any financial instrument can only fall as far as zero, thereby limiting your maximum loss absolutely, theoretically the price of a financial instrument can go on rising forever "to infinity, and beyond" before the force of financial gravity inevitably brings it crashing back to earth.

As a result, top fishing arguably requires you to pay even more attention to risk management through prudent position sizing and the effective use of stop orders. Or to use an alternative trading vehicle that fixes your risk absolutely, like the BetOnMarkets fixed-odds binary bets.

Trend Following

The opposite of bottom (or top) fishing is trend following, as best described by Michael Covel's book titled Trend Following. Rather than betting on a falling price reversing, you bet on a rising price continuing to rise; or a falling price continuing to fall. The trick with trend-following is to buy on the counter-trend dips but in the direction of the major trend, as shown on the following chart.

It is easy to see how buying the FTSE index at any or all of the marked points between July 2010 and February 2011 would have been profitable. But beware: *the trend is your friend only until it ends!*

The following chart shows how betting in line with the FTSE rising trend between 2004 and 2007 would have been profitable, providing you sold out (or even sold short) when the trend reversed and the price broke through the rising trend line in 2007.

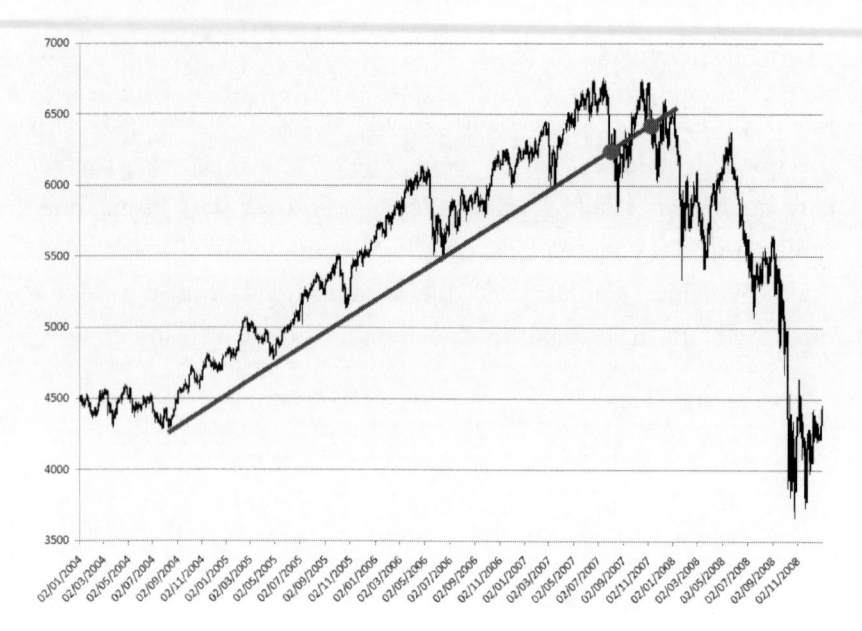

This is a good graphic example of how blindly buying and holding (as many investors do) in the face of adverse price action may be futile... and even downright dangerous.

Bottom Fishing and Trend Following Combined

My own personal approach to position trading is to combine bottom fishing with trend following. In the combined approach I would establish very small exploratory positions in stocks that I think may have fallen too far and are about to reverse, with a few to pyramiding those positions up to meaningful stakes in line with the rising trend when it becomes apparent.

Resistance becomes Support (and vice versa)

First a couple of definitions:

- **Support** is a level at which the price of a financial instrument is more likely to rebound upwards because it finds "support" in the market.

- **Resistance** is a level at which the price of a financial instrument is more likely to rebound downwards because it meets "resistance" in the market.

In the following chart I have used horizontal lines to show the price *support* levels for this particular financial instrument. Wait a minute, no! In the following chart I have used horizontal lines to show the price *resistance* levels for this particular financial instrument. And that's my point here, as will be explained after you've looked at the chart.

My point is that in some cases a previous resistance level (above which the price is unlikely to rise), once broken, becomes a new support level (below which the price is unlikely to fall).

The phenomenon may be useful not only in timing the entry into a new position but also the placement of protective stop orders on new and existing positions – at just below the prior resistance (now anticipated support) level.

For "short" traders the support / resistance phenomenon may also operate in reverse whereby a prior support level (through which the price is unlikely to fall) becomes a new resistance level (through which the price is unlikely to rise).

Nicolas Darvas and his Box Theory

In the 1950s, dancer-turned-speculator Nicolas Darvas devised a "box theory" of how stock prices move; in particular how those prices transition from one trading range to another (higher or lower) trading range. In the following redrawing of the previous chart I have overlaid some potential "Darvas boxes" based on the support / resistance levels shown on the earlier chart.

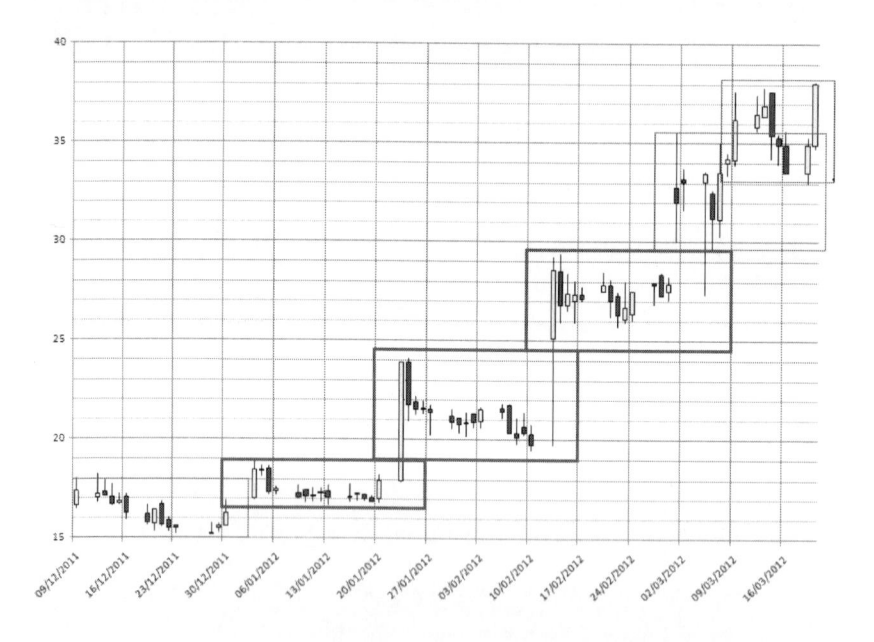

The thick-lined boxes illustrate convincing transitions from one trading range to another whereas the thin-lined boxes illustrate less convincing transitions when the boxes overlap. This overlapping of Darvas boxes may indicate the breakdown of the prevailing price trend.

This story of how Nicolas Darvas devised his box theory is fully documented in the book How I Made $2 Million in the Stock Market (see goo.gl/e9COc).

Moving Average Crossovers

A popular opportunity-identification technique used by traders and investors is the moving average crossover. Before I present an example, some definitions will be useful:

- A "moving average" is simply the average price recorded over the past N days, and it serves to smooth out some of the price volatility so that you can more clearly see the overall trend. The longer the number of days that are averaged, the smoother the line, and the longer the price trend that is being indicated.

- A "moving average crossover" is the point at which the line indicating a shorter moving average (e.g. the 20-day MA) crosses upwards through the line indicating a longer moving average (e.g. the 50-day MA).

In the example that follows, you will see how a moving average crossover trading strategy might work, and also how it might fail if you don't understand the "lagging" nature of moving averages.

Moving Average Crossover Example

In the following contrived (so that it shows what I want it to show) example based on a real price chart, you can see how selling short at labelled point 1, then buying net long at labelled point 2, then selling out at labelled point 3 would have generated some nice profits. These were the points at which the 20-day moving average crossed upwards and downwards through the 50-day moving average, indicating a change of trend.

Hardy Oil & Gas

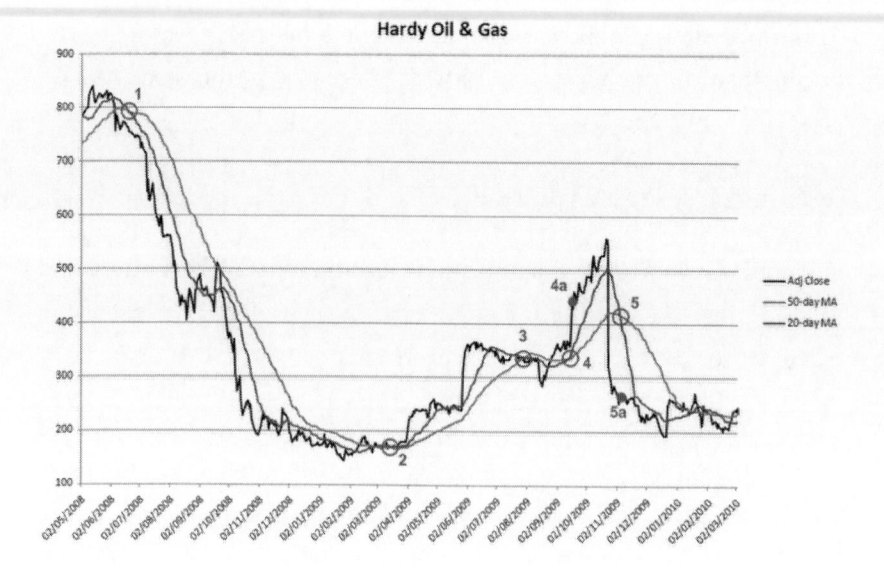

I have chosen the 20-day and 50-day moving averages retrospectively in this case, because with perfect hindsight I know that they produced profitable crossovers. Choosing the right combination of moving averages in advance with imperfect foresight is rather more difficult and there is not necessarily a foolproof one-size-fits-all solution. And there's another problem too...

Judging from the labelled points 4 and 5 you would think at first glance that those too would have been profitable crossovers. Look again; noting that at the time of those crossovers the market prices – labelled as 4a and 5a – were much different from the crossover prices. By buying on the crossover signal 4 (at price 4a, about 450p-per-share) and then selling on crossover signal 5 (at price 5a, about 270p-per-share) you would have succeeded in buying high and selling low despite the crossovers themselves giving the appearance of buying low and selling high.

Moving Average Fans

I know of traders who do use moving average crossovers successfully as part of their trading strategies. Their success seems to hinge on using moving averages as one indicator among many rather than trading solely on the basis of a moving average signal.

These fans of moving averages also tend to look out for various moving averages fanning out from a point, so they might (for example) take a trade when the 20-day MA has risen above the 50-day MA which in turn his risen above the 200-day MA. This kind of signal may be most effective on even shorter timescales and on highly liquid non-equity markets like foreign exchange (forex) currency pairs.

Trading the News

Some spread betting companies and financial web sites encourage you to make stock trading and investment decisions based on the flow of news, but some people assert that you simply can't "trade the news" because:

- The news might already be reflected in the price such that the price might go the wrong way or not move at all when you actually get to read the news.

- By the time you hear the news, you're already too late because someone else will always get the news first.

Prediction is Futile

If you had had some "inside knowledge" about the health of Steve Jobs, how would you have bet on Apple shares just before he died? Short, I reckon. Yet when the great man did die, the Apple share price actually went up.

More recently, on 24 May 2012 I read this headline on the BBC News web site front page: "Mothercare pushed into loss by UK business". What do you think the share price promptly did? That's right; it shot up by more than 12% rather than going down on this ostensibly "bad news".

Prediction is futile because a) we don't know what will happen, and b) we don't know how a share price will react when it does.

Reaction to Over-Reaction May Be More Profitable

I have had some success in "trading the news" in contrary fashion after seeing how the market reacts to the news. If bad news causes a share price to gap-down, I would be more likely to bet on a short-term bounce-back than on a continued fall. And then to switch sides and bet on a resumption of the fall once the rebounding price has retraced to close say 50% of the gap.

I have noticed that the fall-rise-fall pattern or the opposite rise-fall-rise pattern tends to play out over a couple of days, perhaps as a result of longer-term investors (and people with day jobs) reacting to the news a day later than the day traders.

The following chart shows how we could not have predicted on Friday 8 June that the FTSE 100 index would "gap up" on Monday 11 June as a result of the news that Spain had secured massive bank bailout over the weekend. But we might have *reacted* to the news and the price gap by *selling short* on the basis that the gap might close as soon as the initial euphoria had abated and reality had set in.

FTSE 100 chart courtesy of Google Finance

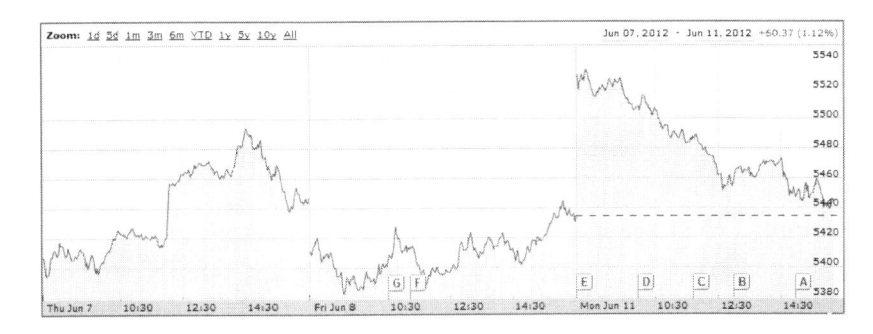

Chapter Summary

In this chapter I have reviewed some of my mainly-technical methods for identifying trading opportunities. In doing so, I have attempted to concentrate on what I think really works and not to simply replicate the existing – and overly complex – trading literature.

8 – One More Thing...

I took inspiration for this chapter's title from Steve Jobs. Not directly, of course.

Although I'm not a big user of Apple Inc. technology – nice though it is – I learned from Walter Isaacson's book Steve Jobs: The Exclusive Biography that he (Steve, not Walter) used to end all of his new product presentations with the phrase "One more thing...", whereupon he would reveal the pièce de résistance product or other showpiece of the presentation.

I also had in the back of my mind an investment book that I had once read, which I think must have been John Mauldin's book Just One Thing: Twelve of the World's Best Investors Reveal the One Strategy You Can't Overlook (see goo.gl/dKsvq).

So I posed one simple question to some experienced spread betting author-publishers and spread companies. The question was: If you could give just one piece of advice to a spread bettor, what would it be?

Disclaimer

One or more of the respondents asked me to include the following disclaimer in relation to their statement(s):

The provision of this content is for general informational purposes only and nothing in this article should be construed as providing investment advice or a solicitation to purchase or sell any investment.

Now on with the show...

Malcolm Pryor

Malcolm is editor of the web site www.spreadbettingcentral.co.uk and author of the best selling spread betting book The Financial Spread Betting Handbook (see goo.gl/op3r9). He says:

My one recommendation to spread bettors is to respect the trend of the instrument they are trading; on the timeframe they are trading it. For instance: in a bear market the majority of spread bettors using daily charts are still trying to find an excuse to go long of stocks, looking for "bargains", and they tend to fight the overall market trend until they run out of money.

Malcolm's tip is particularly resonant with me because, in a sense, he is describing my predominant position trading spread betting style. As such, this piece of advice serves as a good counter-balance and sanity check for some of the material you have read in this book. The one crucial difference (I hope) is that I won't run out of money before the big contrarian wins come – because I practice *prudent position sizing* initially and then *pyramiding with the trend*.

Robbie Burns (aka The Naked Trader)

Many of you will already have heard of Robbie Burns, the trading diarist at www.nakedtrader.co.uk and author of the book The Naked Trader's Guide to Spread Betting (see goo.gl/w6C3U). Robbie initially offered this piece of advice:

Don't tell your wife how much you lost spread betting as she will ****ing kill you!

He was joking, of course, or was he? Either way, he also provided this tip:

Never ever get tempted into spread betting Forex. Nearly everyone loses over time. Yes, that will include you. The only ones to make money out of it are those selling you Forex "systems". Oh, and the spread betting firms of course. You will be bombarded with ads for Forex winning strategies. Don't fall for it.

I am inclined to agree with Robbie about Forex trading, and in this book my preference for spread betting equities will have been obvious, but I know that some of my other responders would likely disagree with both of us. In one sense I think that any financial instrument with a fluctuating price can be successfully (or not so successfully) spread bet and therefore the perceived problem may be with Forex "systems" rather than with Forex markets.

Pete "Monkey with a Pin" Comley

Pete Comley is author of the investment-myth-debunking book Monkey with a Pin at www.monkeywithapin.com. He said:

On the face of it spread betting might have some benefits for the average investor. In my book I show that the average investor loses around 6% a year in three ways: costs, survivorship bias and poor skill. Spread betting gets around the key parts of that 6% by largely removing the cost element e.g. trading commissions, stamp duty, large bid/offer spreads, taxes and account charges. As spread betting is normally short term trading, it does not suffer from survivorship bias either. However the billion dollar question is: what is the average skill of a spread bettor?

A recent Cass Business School report shows that only 20% of futures traders manage to beat the market. That is a pretty low statistic and I would guess that amateur spread betters do much worse on average. I don't see how you can be more successful than the (failing) professional futures traders over a period of time despite your savings on the costs.

My advice is similar to that of Robbie Burns (aka the Naked Trader) above – don't spread bet! If you have been lucky enough to be successful to date, then that's great. Take your profits, walk out of the casino, close your account and go buy a yacht.

I have included Pete's response so as to reflect the range of opinions on spread betting, and because I have a lot of respect for the sensible book he has written. I think there is a subtlety in the Naked Trader's referenced advice – which is actually to *not spread bet Forex* specifically rather than to not spread bet at all. If Pete is arguing that all individual investment endeavours are futile, which arguably they might be, then I think this applies no more to spread betting than it does to investing traditionally via a stockbroker share dealing account.

Andy Richardson

Andy Richardson developed the comprehensive spread betting resource web site at www.financial-spread-betting.com. His advice for spread bettors is:

If you are not in a proper frame of mind, don't trade. If you are not prepared, or you are distracted by other activities, stay out of the market until you can again concentrate on the business of trading. Secondly, guard against burnout. Any pursuit which demands so much leads to occasional burnout. Learn to recognize the signs of burnout in yourself. When you feel burned out, look to close all of your trading positions. Your judgement will be impaired, and you risk your most important asset – your self-confidence. Step back until you regain perspective.

As someone who writes and publishes while simultaneously operating accounts with one or more of the spread betting companies, this response resonates with me. It was a real problem for me some years ago when trying to "day trade" during the hour from 8am to 9am (and perhaps at lunch time too) while also trying to hold down a regular job with an employer. It is less of a problem now that I have a longer position trading timeframe and now that I have full control over my own time.

TRADERS' Magazine

A representative from TRADERS' Magazine at www.tradersonline-mag.com offered the following advice to spread bettors:

Putting risk first is paramount. We interviewed many great traders and almost all of them told us that controlling risk religiously is far more important than actually making money. The latter will take care of itself. Most new traders, however, do not internalise that paradigm, which leads to a high probability of an account blow-up at some point during their career. Do not make that mistake. Be smart. Follow the wisdom of the great traders.

I believe this advice to be entirely consistent with the content of *this book* as well as my Stop Orders and Position Trading books.

Capital Spreads

Angus Campbell, Head of Market Analysis at Capital Spreads (see goo.gl/71Mt0) provided the following simple but profound suggestion:

Don't run your losses!

Allowing a losing position to get worse by moving your stop order further away is a cardinal and common error made by retail clients; one which you would never expect a professional or institutional investor to do.

Our psychology as traders and rational human beings drives us to bite our finger nails and hope (or even pray) that a worsening position will come back in our favour; rather than biting the bullet and cutting the loss. If the market does come back, the temptation is to breathe a huge sigh of relief, close the position for a meagre profit, and congratulate ourselves on having done so well to avoid a £1,000 loss and actually realise a £10 profit. It sounds logical, but is not good risk management.

I've said pretty much the same thing at various points in *this book*, but it was well worth Angus saying it again. Opening yourself up to the possible loss of £1,000 for every £10 profit that you bank is definitely not good risk-reward ratio.

SpreadEx

David White of spread betting company SpreadEx (see goo.gl/9uOvr) answered the "one more thing" question as follows.

When looking to spread bet a trading idea, research the product to determine the asset's normalised volatility relative to the broader market – i.e. its beta.

Using as much leverage as your provider will allow will magnify the volatility of a historically volatile instrument, to the point that it becomes unmanageable. High gearing could result in your position being closed through lack of funds from only a small change in price, regardless of whether the trade proves profitable over your set time horizon. Conversely, gearing up by using leverage on a less volatile instrument can help you generate bigger returns from smaller price moves (relative to the broader market) while still meeting the demands of your risk profile.

If spread bettors can differentiate between products which are inherently volatile and those that aren't, then the ability to both see a trading idea through and to maximise capital efficiency with an appropriate use of leverage will supplement trading success with a more robust and empirical understanding of risk management.

I have to admit that when thinking about the possible answers to my "one more thing" question, I hadn't even thought of this one.

InterTrader

Steve Ruffley, an Education Consultant at InterTrader (see goo.gl/AXwob) said:

The words spread betting implies that there is a gamble and element of luck in trading, but in my experience trading the markets profitably cannot be further away from the action of gambling. Investing in your education so as to understand how fundamental news moves the markets and how technical patterns and levels lead to self-fulfilling market movements will not only give you the tools and knowledge to trade but also the confidence to be profitable. Trading with confidence and with pre-defined goals and stops is how to profit from trading; if you fail to plan in trading, you are inevitably planning to fail.

We would expect an education consultant to stress the importance of trading education, wouldn't we? But since the most if not all spread betting companies provide free education resources, I don't see this as self-serving.

SVSFX Securities

Kulvir Virk, CEO of SVS Securities Plc which operates the MetaTrader broker SVSFX (see goo.gl/xxarA) offered the following advice:

As a broker we get to see many different trading strategies from many different types of client. Whilst we offer high leverage, 1:400 in some cases, this is a maximum which should be used carefully with close attention to money management. We see clients with good trade ideas losing on the back of playing too big, because even an excellent trader or excellent trading system could lose 10 or 20 trades in a row. Money management must account for the worst case scenario, and I would say that this is at least 50% of the basis of a good trading plan.

This advice reinforces my decision to cover money- and risk-management in this book before contemplating the identification of trading opportunities.

Chapter Summary

When I posed the question "If you could give just one piece of advice to a spread bettor, what would it be?" I half-expected some of the responders to proffer their top tips for *winning big*. I should have known better, because if there is one thing that seasoned spread bettors can agree on it is this:

You must be careful, and manage your risk.

One way or another, all of the responses reflect this safety-first ethos.

Now let me offer my own answer to the question I posed. My answer is:

Don't be an Average Frustrated Chump (AFC)!

In his best-selling book titled The Game, Neil Strauss talks about AFCs: Average Frustrated Chumps. These are the real-life regular guys who chase girls desperately in order to get dates, usually with little success. The spread world is also populated with Average Frustrated Chumps who chase stocks desperately out of fear of "missing out".

With girls (or boys) and stocks a more relaxed attitude often pays off. There's plenty more fish in the sea so if you love it, let it go. If it's right for you, it will come back. And they very often do.

One More Thing...

Oh, and one more thing:

In this book I have advised at all times to bet small, often starting with the minimum stake allowed by your chosen spread betting company. Yet I am also mindful of one piece of advice given in Max Gunther's book The Zurich Axioms, which is to "always play for meaningful stakes".

Meaningful stakes are, of course, relative to the person doing the playing. A brand new spread bettor of ordinary means would be wise to deposit no more than £1,000 initially; or maybe start with £1500 divided between three different spread betting companies. A multimillionaire would no doubt feel rather silly playing with any less than tens of thousands of pounds.

Whether you are a regular Joe or a high roller, one thing is paramount. Deploy your deposited cash – however meaningful – across many parallel positions or between several serial trades... and never bet the farm on one throw of the dice!

Have fun and be careful when Better Spread Betting, and don't forget to tune into the web site at www.betterspreadbetting.com.

Appendix – Spread Betting Resources

In this appendix you will find links to useful additional resources that will help you become a better spread bettor. This information comprises a selection of spread betting companies that I have used and which are mentioned in this book, contracts for difference (CFD) providers and other trading platform providers, and inspirational spread betting and trading books.

This information is given in good faith, with no liability accepted by the author or publisher.

Spread Betting Companies

Here is a selection of the spread betting companies that I have used and which are mentioned in this book. They are arranged roughly into my order of preference at the time of writing, but of course it's entirely your decision as to which one (or ones) you choose.

Capital Spreads, visit goo.gl/71Mt0
IG Index, visit goo.gl/uJ3NQ
InterTrader, visit goo.gl/AXwob
ETX Capital, visit goo.gl/eVLLI

SpreadEx, visit goo.gl/9uOvr
Financial Spreads, visit goo.gl/xnfn0

You can access my list of spread betting companies and read my latest opinions of them at:

www.betterspreadbetting.com/p/companies.html

Contracts for Difference (CFD) Providers

Contracts for difference (CFD) trading accounts are offered by many spread betting companies as an alternative to spread betting. They may be of particular interest to those who are not eligible to trade via spread betting in their jurisdiction, e.g. in the United States.

Besides the spread betting companies themselves, some providers specialise only in CFD trading. For example:

Plus500, visit goo.gl/IMUBX

Other Trading Platform Providers

Bet On Markets (visit goo.gl/uiime) provides an alternative to traditional spread betting in the form of fixed-odds binary bets.

SVSFX Securities (visit goo.gl/xxarA) provides a subtly different form of spread betting known as margin trading.

Spread Betting Books

The best financial spread betting books to date (apart from this one) are Malcolm Pryor's books:

The Financial Spread Betting Handbook (see goo.gl/op3r9), Winning Spread Betting Strategies (see goo.gl/A0m0G), and 7 Charting Tools for Spread Betting (see goo.gl/yYKQ0).

For those looking to move to the next level, Malcolm has also produced some instructional DVDs including Malcolm Pryor's Spread Betting Techniques (see goo.gl/dE1GV) and Malcolm Pryor on Short Term Spread Betting (see goo.gl/yVnR9).

Robbie Burns, the original Naked Trader, also has an introductory spread betting book titled (unsurprisingly) The Naked Trader's Guide to Spread Betting (see goo.gl/w6C3U).

Inspirational Trading Books

I hope you'll find my other books about Position Trading (see goo.gl/KfRH2) and Stop Orders (see goo.gl/hvxAj) to be both inspirational and complementary to this book.

Of the many trading books I have read over the years, just a few have remained on my trading bookshelf as lasting inspirations. They are Reminiscences of a Stock Operator (see goo.gl/uLvGa), How I Made $2 Million in the Stock Market (see goo.gl/e9COc), Trend Following (see goo.gl/RPldT), and Trade Your Way to Financial Freedom (see goo.gl/4iymP).

Also by Tony Loton

Published by Harriman House

Stop Orders: A practical guide to using stop orders, for traders and investors at goo.gl/hvxAj

A stop order is an essential tool used for money management and risk limitation, but for many investors and traders it is not terribly well understood.

This book covers everything you need to know about stop orders and how to make them work for you. Whether you are a trader, an investor, or a spread bettor, you should regard the stop order as essential in helping you lock in your profits and succeed in the markets.

Published by LOTONtech

Position Trading: BUY like a Trader and HOLD like an Investor at goo.gl/KfRH2

You have no doubt heard the phrase "a long-term investment is a short-term trade gone bad", meaning that when a stock falls in price soon after purchase we tend to hold on 'for the long term' in the hope of a recovery. This book turns that phrase on its head by presenting the position trader's mantra: "a long-term investment is a short-term trade gone well".

The End

This is the last printed page of the book. If additional blank pages have been added by the printer, rest assured that you have not missed anything, and you can use the additional pages to make your own notes.

www.betterspreadbetting.com